Advance praise for CONFUSION TO CLARITY

"*Confusion to Clarity* is an insightful exploration of twenty-somethings today that sheds light on why this decade can be so difficult for Gen Y. Ann speaks to the reader from a place of knowledge, experience, and understanding, and helps each person to discover what their calling in life is. This is a great resource for twentysomethings who are trying to get to the true core of who they are." Christine Hassler
Life coach and author of *20 Something*
20 Everything and *20 Something Manifesto*

"One of life's most challenging questions is undoubtedly, 'What gives my life true meaning and purpose?' The gift of this book is that it offers guidance for successfully pursuing answers to that question. Like a guide who has been into the wilderness herself, the author provides tools with real depth to help readers forge their own paths. Beautifully written and drawn from solid experience, this book is a *must-read*." Hal Zina Bennett
Author of *Write from the Heart:*
Unleashing the Power of Your Creativity

"Ann Elizabeth Grace has written an indispensable resource for young people that yearn to passionately follow their true callings. *Confusion to Clarity* is insightful, enlightening and, best of all, exceptionally action-oriented. Ms. Grace's readers can start to see results quite quickly if they apply even a fraction of her well-heeled recommendations. In fact, this book is not only relevant to readers in their twenties, but to persons of any age who are at a crossroads of what to do with their lives. I simply cannot heap enough praise on this much-needed book for its practical and honest guidance on being a twentysomething in the twenty-first century." David A. Morrison
President of TWENTYSOMETHING™ Inc./
Global Consulting & Research, and
author of *Marketing to the Campus Crowd*

"Ann Grace does an excellent job illustrating that everybody has their own calling in life. The choice is whether to pursue this calling or not. Most times, it requires trial and error, taking risks, following your heart, and listening to your inner thoughts. The first step is learning how to take a step back and understand what motivates and pulls you. *Confusion to Clarity* explains exactly how to do that. The rest is up to you!"

Lee Wellman
Author of *My Quarter-Life Crisis:*
How an Anxiety Disorder Knocked Me
Down, and How I Got Back Up

"Ann Grace says in her book … that every generation struggles to grow up, but the offspring of Baby Boomers have unique challenges, chief of which is getting over the fear that they will not live up to unrealistic parental and societal expectations. Using her own and peers' stories, and a great deal of compassion and intelligence, she shows her generation how to navigate the often painful but ultimately rewarding journey to meaningful work."

Nancy Anderson
Author of *Work with Passion: How*
to Do What You Love for a Living

CONFUSION
to CLARITY

The Twentysomething's Guide
to Finding Your Calling

ANN ELIZABETH GRACE

Confusion to Clarity: The Twentysomething's
Guide to Finding Your Calling

Published by Wheatmark®
610 East Delano Street, Suite 104
Tucson, Arizona 85705 U.S.A.
www.wheatmark.com

International Standard Book Number:
978-1-60494-326-9

Library of Congress Control Number:
2009932941

Contents

Part 4
Relationships

Part 5
Tools

Note: some names of interview subjects have been changed for privacy purposes.

Preface

"The Odyssey Years." The *New York Times* columnist David Brooks uses this expression to depict the new life stage of today's twenties, and he describes it as "the decade of wandering that frequently occurs between adolescence and adulthood."[1] During the odyssey years, we drift through various jobs, relationships, cities, and educational programs—our finances often in disarray. Although such rootlessness is exciting, the flip side is that it can also be very unsettling. Triggered by high expectations and the perpetual uncertainty surrounding our present and future circumstances, many of us tumble into depression, anxiety, and plummeting self-esteem.

Media images and assumptions from older generations sometimes stereotype twentysomethings as self-absorbed people who are only interested in dating, having fun on the weekends, and becoming rich and famous. But I believe we carry deeper concerns that are often overlooked. Beneath the ups and downs of our daily lives, we are seeking purpose, direction, and the knowledge that we are serving the world around us. We want to know who we are on the inside, grow as individuals, and actively apply our gifts in a unique and meaningful way. When these elements are lacking, malaise creeps in. This book peels back the layers of twentysome-thing life to address the underlying themes of meaning and purpose.

I wrote *Confusion to Clarity* after I had finally begun to come to terms with who I am and what I want to do in the world. For me, this book originated from the suffering—and tremendous personal growth—that have come to define this stage of life. It is now clear to me that the painful turmoil we endure during our twenties ultimately helps us grow to new heights and depths. After all of the confusion, heartache, and restlessness, we reach a point of surrender. This is the point at which we understand that none of the voices outside will ever lead us to enduring happiness. It is the point at which we connect to the quiet, wise voice of our inner self, ask our questions, and listen to the answers. It is the path that leads us to our calling.

The main goal of *Confusion to Clarity* is to provide you with emotional support for traversing the peaks and valleys of your twenties. A theme that weaves through almost all of the chapters is that of work. This is inevitable because figuring out what we want to do as a career colors every aspect of this decade. You'll also find many practical tips that you can apply to your own search. To stimulate your reflective process, I have included many questions and exercises. You may want to write in a journal as you come to each one, or skim all of them and reflect later on the ones that speak most strongly to you. Or just read them through once or twice and let them gestate in your mind.

This book is also the product of many hours of listen-ing. To create it, I conducted interviews with over two dozen people in their twenties and thirties. They generously shared with me their joys and struggles in order to provide you—the reader—with ideas for how to navigate your twenties. All of the stories in this book are true, and even though some are long and some are short, they all offer unique insight. As a result of my conversations with others, I have had the privilege of viewing my generation not only as a member, but also as an observer. My interview subjects have continually inspired me with their spark, talent, intelligence, and heart. By witnessing their hunger to evolve and contribute to the greater good of our world, I have been changed for the better. I may not have all the answers, but I have grown immeasurably by delving into the questions.

I hope you enjoy mulling over the stories, ideas, and exercises woven throughout these pages and apply their insights to your life in ways that feel right for you. I would love to hear about your own journey, so please contact me through www.annelizabethgrace.com. In the meantime, I wish you happiness and much success.

Ann Grace

Twentysomethings Today

I was huddled in the utility closet on my dorm floor, crying softly into the phone to my dad. Trying to ignore the buoyant sounds of footsteps and girls' laughter penetrating through the door, I said, "Something's wrong with me, Dad. I'm trying to settle in and have fun, but I don't want to be here." I whimpered quietly so as not to alert my peers to the truth of my sudden plunge into depression. "I'm pretending to be okay, but I'm *not*."

Soon after arriving at college, I was struck by a frightening, pervasive sense of free-fall. I had weathered my share of storms growing up and thought of myself as strong and independent. But suddenly I didn't know who I was or what I wanted, much less how I was ever going to get there. This was hardly what I expected after a lifetime of being pumped up by society with catch phrases like: "You can have it all" and "You can be whatever you want when you grow up." My personal favorite was: "Anything is possible."

Long weeks turned into long months in which my loved ones' persistent attempts to comfort me were unsuccessful. I plastered a smile on my face that was carefully designed to hide my grief and my shame. After all, college was supposed to be one of the best times of my life, and I knew I was privileged just to be there. Yet I was drowning in loneliness, confusion, and anxiety. Morning found me struggling to get out of bed, often with silent tears rolling down my cheeks. Evenings found me trying to fit in and hide the pain I felt inside. Even my physical body hurt: I ached from head to toe and lost my appetite.

Publicly I smiled; privately I cried. Publicly I performed; privately I ached. If only I had known then how many of my peers were also suffering, I might not have felt so alone. But at the time I met few who acknowledged—much less discussed in depth—their anxiety or depression. Maybe they, like me, didn't know how to.

If you were born between the late 1970s and the mid-1990s, there is a strong possibility that you can relate to my experience. Because we are still young and generations are largely defined in hindsight, experts have so far failed to reach a consensus about the exact birth dates that define us. In fact, they're not even sure what to call us. The choice of descriptions includes the Millennials, Echo Boomers, Generation Next, ADD Generation, MTV Generation, and Generation Me. For the purposes of this book, I have chosen to use the term "Generation Y."

As members of the "Y" generation, we are the children of the Baby Boomers (1946–1964) and the younger siblings of the Gen Xers (1965–1976). Roughly 75 million strong,[2] we are the largest generation since that of our parents, and approximately 39 million of us are in our twenties.[3] Gen Yers are a globally aware and diverse group; only 61 percent of us identify as "white."[4] We are also a highly educated generation: 64 percent of women and 60 percent of men head to college after graduating from high school, and 85 percent attend full time.[5]

Anxiety and Depression

Despite such positive statistics, Gen Yers also experience high levels of anxiety and depression. In their *New York Times* best-selling book, *Quarterlife Crisis*, authors Alexandra Robbins and Abby Wilner detail the common struggles twentysomethings face as they transition into adulthood. In researching their book, the authors discovered a void in concrete statistics focused specifically on the mental health of twentysomethings. However, they interviewed more than one hundred people in this age group and uncovered a pervasive sense of confusion, self-doubt, and emotional turmoil triggered by the dramatic changes human beings undergo during this stage of life.[6]

I, too, had a difficult time finding mental health statistics about twentysomethings when conducting research for this book. To gain insight into the widespread themes and issues facing those of us who are moving through this decade, I read many books and articles and talked with my peers. In the end, I reached conclusions that are similar to those of Robbins and Wilner: bouts of depression and anxiety, as well as feelings of being lost, are very common among twentysomethings.

The absence of research focused specifically on the psychological state of twentysomethings is unfortunate. However, in recent years numerous studies have been conducted on the mental health of college students. While I recognize that not all twentysomethings attend or graduate from college, I will present some of the findings here because this data focuses on people who are typically in or approaching their twenties. Hopefully this information will shed light on some of the pressures twentysomethings face.

In 2007, a student at Virginia Tech University murdered 32 students and faculty on campus before taking his own life. After the tragedy, *Newsweek* magazine reported, "By all accounts, schools are dealing with more students with emotional problems than ever." In 2001 psychiatrists in the University of Virginia's counseling office had 24 one-hour appointments available each week; in 2007 they had 80.[7] A 2007 survey by the American College Health Association found that at one or more times within the last 12 months, 56 percent of men and 65 percent of women reported feeling "things were hopeless," 38 percent of men and 46 percent of women reported feeling "so depressed that it was difficult to function," and 86 percent of men and 95 percent of women reported feeling "overwhelmed" by all they had to do.[8]

Human nature dictates that emotions find an outlet. When anxiety and depression become too painful to address directly, some people turn to drugs and alcohol for relief. According to a report by The National Center on Addiction and Substance Abuse at Columbia University, "Each month, half (49.4 percent) of all full-time college students ages 18-22 binge drink, abuse prescription drugs and/or abuse illegal drugs." In 2005, nearly 23 percent of these college students met the medical criteria for substance abuse or dependence. And the proportion of college students who abuse alcohol, prescription drugs, and illegal drugs has risen dramatically since the mid-1990s.[9]

As emotional challenges become increasingly difficult to manage, some twentysomethings seek therapy and/or take antidepressants. Some project their turmoil outward, fueling constant relationship dramas or engaging in risky behaviors. Others withdraw from family and friends. Still others develop more insidious traits including perfectionism, obsessive-compulsive tendencies, and body-image distortions and eating disorders. Sadly, according to the National Institute of Mental Health, in 2004 suicide was the third leading cause of death among young adults ages 20–24.[10]

Early Influences

Where does our turmoil come from? Let's start with the big picture. Like all generations, we have been heavily influenced by our parents' generation, who carved out many of the cultural norms we now take for granted. Unwilling to accept the status quo in their youth, the Baby Boomers challenged rigid family dynamics, social injustice, racial prejudice, workplace inequality, religious dogma, and hypocrisy. They ushered in a new cultural era alongside television's shift from black-and-white to color. As traditional institutions and ideologies crumbled, the assassination of some of their most powerful and influential leaders (President John F. Kennedy, Martin Luther King, Jr., Robert Kennedy, and John Lennon) left them shattered.

Some of our fathers resisted fighting in the Vietnam War to the tune of "Hell no! We won't go!" At the same time, many of our mothers were fighting for their rightful place as equals in society. As the glass ceiling came into closer view, Helen Reddy's song, "I Am Woman," won a Grammy and became an anthem for the feminist movement of the 1970s. Gender roles went up in flames along with our mothers' bras.

In addition to playing a pivotal role in the larger social dramas of the '60s, '70s, and '80s, our parents started a new mass movement by embarking on a journey of self-discovery, of healing the "inner child" and finding their "authentic selves." The efforts of many Boomers to replace religiosity with a devotion to personal growth led to an abundance of spiritual gurus, psychological theories, and transformational workshops—not to mention talk show royalty like Phil Donahue and Oprah Winfrey.

Collectively, the Baby Boomers had blazed such an unprecedented trail that by the time they got married and had children, they had earned the right to instill in us the notion of "The sky's the limit." Inherent in their mentoring was a focus on boosting our self-esteem so we would never have to feel stifled by the restrictions that had been placed on previous generations. Regardless of the quality of our performance, we were heralded with gold stars from teachers for completing homework assignments, certificates from piano instructors for participating in recitals, and trophies from coaches for playing in soccer games. And our parents—including many dads who were striving to be more emotionally involved role models than their own fathers had been—captured it all on camera.

In our youth, the notion of "Girl Power" charged to the forefront of pop culture, picking up where our mothers had left off. We belted out "Girls Just Want to Have Fun" with Cyndi Lauper, "Express Yourself" with Madonna, and "I'll tell you what I want, what I really really want…" with the Spice Girls. Television shows featuring strong female characters became huge hits. Joss Whedon, creator of *Buffy the Vampire Slayer*, shed light on this phenomenon when he talked about "the very first mission statement of the show, which was the joy of female power: having it, using it, sharing it."[11]

And so in childhood we smiled and posed, basking in the limelight as buzzwords such as "options," "possibilities," and "opportunities" lingered in the air and pre-paved our limitless destinies. Among parents, teachers, coaches, music instructors, scout troop leaders, the media, extended family members, and family friends, the message "You're special" was instilled in us by at least one adult (if not many) during our formative years. We were all winners, and we liked it that way.

Emotional Wounds

But the going wasn't always easy. Amidst the newfound personal freedom, the foundations of family life were cracking. A large number of our parents' marriages unraveled in divorce, and even children whose families remained intact could not avoid the impact of the crumbling family unit. Many helped friends through the pain of divorce or were caught in the middle of their own family dysfunction. As stress at home bubbled to the surface, some of our parents succumbed to depression, faltering self-esteem, and erratic behavior, which clouded their interactions with us and affected our emotional development.

Like the parents of so many of my peers, my own parents also split up. Despite my outward appearance of success, the inward stress I felt during my formative years shook me to the core just as my sense of self was struggling to emerge. Feelings of instability led me to an impossible quest for perfection. Lacking the maturity to heal my emotional wounds, unconsciously I thought that if I could just do everything *right*, I would finally be "okay." Although I was surrounded by many loving, caring people, at times I was locked in a fog of confusion. I became an excellent listener to the people around me, but I struggled to listen to myself. Without a strong sense of self to fall back on, it's no wonder I crumbled the first time I tried to embark into the world on my own.

Millions of Gen Yers have similar stories to tell. The erosion of our self-confidence is particularly ironic given the vast amounts of self-esteem with which we were showered. Some of us lost our way at home, perhaps due to stifling parental expectations, emotional/sexual/physical abuse, family alcoholism, drug addiction, mental illness, physical disability, fear-based religious dogma, or the death of a family member. Others of us lost our way outside as we were bullied and rejected by our peers, taunted with prejudice, or pressured to fit in. Some of us struggled to come to terms with our gender or sexual orientation. And sometimes the confusing hormonal changes that occurred in our rapidly changing bodies were enough to send us into a tailspin.

As twentysomethings, we have the responsibility now to put all of these events into perspective. Every generation struggles to grow up, and it is through facing and overcoming challenges that we learn. It is also important to acknowledge that most of our parents, guardians, and community members did the best job they could in raising us. Despite such truths, it is also critical that we become aware of the emotional baggage we acquired in our youth—at an age in which we may have lacked the tools to understand or overcome it. Many of us have carried this baggage with us into our twenties, and it is essential now that we begin to heal.

Economic Strain

After high school many of us went on to college, filled with hopes and dreams about the future. But when we left college, with or without a diploma, it was common to have mixed feelings due to the financial obligations we had incurred. According to the book *Generation Debt*, nearly two-thirds of U.S. college students borrow money to pay for school. Studies in 2004 and 2005 estimated that the average student loan debt for graduates of four-year colleges was between $17,600 and $23,485.[12]

And those are just the costs of a basic undergraduate education. When you toss in all of the additional debt from credit cards and graduate or professional school, the number rises rapidly. In addition to our financial strain is the frustrating realization that even with our expensive degrees, competition for well-paying jobs with solid benefits is stiff.

Adding even more pressure to these challenges is the fact that employer-sponsored retirement plans have become more important than ever in the face of Social Security's uncertain future. Unfortunately, many Gen Yers (college-educated or not) have temporary jobs, work part-time, or are employed by companies that offer no benefits—retirement or otherwise. In fact, *Generation Debt* reveals that "About 30 percent of Americans aged nineteen to twenty-nine consistently have no health insurance, double the percentage of the population at large, and more than any other age group."

Our generation is also facing worldwide structural economic changes that have made it notably more difficult for us to gain entry into the middle class than it was for our parents and grandparents. As the gap between rich and poor grows wider, many of us are left struggling to find firm financial ground as we step into the "real world" and try to make it on our own.

Anyone Can Be Famous

As we were growing up, the fast-paced era of Internet technology, cell phones, and reality TV arrived in full force. Suddenly we were instantly connected—not only to our own families and friends, but also quite literally to the whole world. We quickly adapted to these changes and began marking our territory in cyberspace by creating blogs, websites, YouTube videos, and MySpace and Facebook pages.

One of the most striking results of such cutting-edge technology was that Gen Yers unconsciously acquired the belief that anyone could become famous. This set a new bar by which many of us came to measure success: doing something that brings us public recognition. David Morrison, of the consulting and research firm Twentysomething Inc., says:

> The twenty-first century has been defined, in part, by the common person being famous for merely being himself (or herself). Look no further than such shows as *The Hills, The Real Housewives of Orange County, Survivor,* and *Big Brother.* Regular people, simply broadcasting their daily lives to millions of viewers, can become celebrities in their own right. Sponsorship and book deals are becoming par for the course. This trend represents a completely new paradigm shift in entertainment, and it's having a profound crossover effect on the attitudes and behaviors of today's teens and young adults.

Today the media spotlight shines brightly on rich, famous, and beautiful celebrities. I once heard a woman attribute the success of *American Idol* to the fact that viewers got to watch developing performers. While this was true, it struck me that viewers also projected their own desire for stardom onto these young artists. We tuned in week after week not only to watch fame unfold for the contestants, but also to bear witness to what many of us secretly hope will be our own destiny. At the same time, many of us are troubled by the gap between our ambitions and the reality of our daily lives. As this gap grows wider, in part due to constant media images of affluence and beauty, we feel increasing pressure to meet unrealistically high expectations.

Psychological Toll

When soaring expectations meet unhealed wounds, real-world debt, stiff competition, an overabundance of choices, and the desire for things to happen *now*, many of us start to feel inadequate. After all, the flip side of being a winner is being a loser. Although we are a creative, innovative, and globally aware generation, when the sky's the limit, it's easy to feel like we're not achieving enough no matter what we do.

Emma, twenty-three, summed up this collective experience when she said, "I always get anxious before a birthday because I feel like I haven't accomplished enough for my age." This comes from an impressive young woman who has already earned a college degree, influenced society by working for several nonprofit organizations, and moved from one coast to the other in pursuit of adventure and self-discovery. She is also a talented painter and singer and is preparing for graduate school! If Emma isn't exempt from feelings of inadequacy, who is?

Because the path to adulthood is unclear, many of us feel like we are adrift in a sea of impermanence, constantly grappling with questions about who we are, where we are going, and what our purpose in life is. As a result of the internal confusion, we sometimes shift uncomfortably when other people ask us the age-old question, "What do you want to do with your life?" The truth is that many of us just don't know, even if we already have job experience under our belt and/or have earned a college degree. While trying to stammer out an answer, another portion of our self-esteem crashes. The struggle to become emotionally and financially independent is so common that many twentysomethings move back home for a period of time.

We are privileged to be globally connected and to have opportunities that previous generations lacked, and it's important to be grateful for the options in front of us. Yet we are bombarded with so many sources of information that many of us feel paralyzed. If the food on a buffet table stretches for miles, it's easy to lose touch with what we are hungry for. When so much information floods us from the outside, we can lose touch with who we are on the inside. At times we just want to hide away. Meanwhile we compare ourselves negatively with others: *they* are farther along, more accomplished, more together. So what's the matter with me?

Many of us also feel lonely due to the dramatic changes in our social life after leaving school, as well as our willingness to follow a restless, independent spirit. And if we are not moving around, our friends are. Since close, supportive relationships are a chief component to happiness, it's no wonder that we struggle. We float in and out of friendships and intimate relationships at the same age when our parents and/or grandparents were settling down, getting married, and building long-term community.

Taking a wider view, twentysomethings are also affected by the larger issues facing humanity. In the face of a highly unstable economy, a complex energy crisis, the threat of nuclear weapons, school shootings, domestic and international poverty, environmental degradation, disease epidemics, and terrorism, we teeter on the delicate edge between compassion and helplessness or hopelessness.

Another factor is that by the time we reach our mid-to-late twenties, many of us have lost at least one family member or friend to death. The awareness of our mortality is more powerful than any other realization because it compels us to clarify our priorities and make decisions that will create a legacy we can be proud of. But the ticking of every clock reminds us that time is passing. Many of us feel existential anxiety, even low-grade panic, that we are failing to make our time count fully, failing to uncover and develop the potential buried deep within us.

Self-Discovery

Many Gen Yers have turned to self-discovery to help them navigate through their confusion. I am no exception. Over time, I developed a daily meditation practice; sought therapy; expressed my creativity through writing, painting, and music; started to practice yoga; spent time in nature; and found avenues to be of service to others. Slowly but surely I made peace with myself and came into contact with my true self, which has allowed me to be more available to the world around me.

Since graduating from college, I have bounced around through various cities, states, countries, relationships, and jobs. Along the way, I stumbled into numerous challenges and became intimately acquainted with the uncertainties that loom over this decade. Yet I came to understand that embracing uncertainty was the only way for me to find stability in the face of the unknown. I also came to believe that something good can come out of every experience, no matter how difficult. These new realizations, and my dedication to personal growth, helped to ease the jolts of transition.

In the process, my twenties became a decade of inner transformation. Most important of all, I now know that creating a life I love starts inside myself. Although I have learned to rely on myself, I also know that I do not have to "do it all" alone. As a result, I continue to find supportive people with whom to share my path. When I was mired in depression, I was unaware that my emotional collapse was the beginning of a much larger process that would eventually give way to great joy.

From the vantage point of today, I now look back and feel gratitude for the fact that I fell apart at a young age. Had I not, I likely would have continued on for many more years with a dull, yet tolerable, ache in my heart. Gradually I would have grown accustomed to looking outside for answers that can, in reality, only come from inside myself. Today I understand that the nagging sense of "something missing" points to a frayed connection with my inner voice. Now I have the tools to reconnect with it at will.

At heart we all seek greater meaning in our lives. If we can remain open, we will recognize the "aha moment," the point at which we realize that the answers lie within us. Yes, we do face many external stressors in our twenties, from career and finances to personal relationships, and we need to develop strategies to address them. But the ability to thrive in the midst of challenging situations is dependent on self-discovery. As Alicia, twenty-seven, points out, "When things fall apart on the outside, what do you have on the inside?"

Nothing and no one outside of us will ever be able to accurately assess what we want and tell us how to get it. Outside sources might be able to nudge us along, but lasting happiness will only come when we develop a strong connection to our deepest selves.

A Note about Spirituality

Because this book focuses on personal growth, I and the people I interviewed occasionally use the words "spirit" and "spiritual" to explore various ideas. I also reference concepts that are commonly associated with spirituality such as *true self, inner voice, energy, meditation,* and, of course, *calling.* The notion of spirituality means different things to different people. Naturally, it draws widely varying responses. For some, it triggers a positive and uplifting feeling. For others, it triggers a negative impression ranging from skepticism and doubt to outright rejection. We each have different backgrounds and thought processes that inform our views, and all views are welcome here.

That being said, let me clarify what spirituality means to me. I believe that the core of a spiritual life is about seeking and finding truth and meaning for ourselves. It is a commitment to following the questions of our heart such as: *Who am I? Why am I here? How should I use my talents?* In my experience, spirituality is different from religion. A spiritual person does not need to be religious, although a religious person can certainly be spiritual. I was raised in the Catholic tradition, attended a Buddhist-inspired university, and have studied many world religions. While I do not identify as a member of any religion, my spiritual path is guided by the conviction that we are all equals in the human family; we are connected at the core level; and love is the most powerful energy available to us.

Studies show that many Gen Yers prioritize spiritual growth and are forming their own personalized views about the meaning of life. They are also doing so through more informal means than previous generations. One study found that 80 percent of college students "have an interest in spirituality"; three-fourths say that they are "searching for meaning/ purpose in life" or that they discuss the meaning of life with friends; and nearly half report that they consider it "essential" or "very important" to seek opportunities to help them grow spiritually.[13] Another study found that 35 percent of people between the ages of 18 and 25 describe themselves as "spiritual but not religious."[14]

Spirituality is not a one-size-fits-all experience; it is unique to each individual. For many Gen Yers (religious or not), the core of a spiritual life centers on becoming a better person; creating fulfillment in the everyday arenas of work, relationships, and activities; and the feeling that they are making a positive impact on society. Many of us have incorporated yoga, meditation, prayer, creative pursuits, or service projects into our lives. Others have found a sense of connection through spending time in nature and pondering the meaning of life with family and friends.

Looking Forward

I now understand that it is okay to go through periods of feeling confused, anxious, depressed, overwhelmed, lost, ashamed, and inadequate in your twenties. When you are feeling down, it is important to take good care of yourself, reach out for support, and remember that things will turn around. And if you are really struggling, I also recommend seeking professional help from a therapist, doctor, mentor, or support group.

Over time, as you grapple with your turbulent emotions, you will discover that they are just passing through you and they do not define you. By taking action and trying new things, you will gain more life experience that helps you develop clarity about what you want, as well as confidence in your ability to create it. This process of growth helps you discover who you are and what you have to give. It leads you to a meaningful life that you are proud to call your own, and it leads you to your calling.

Whereas I once associated *calling* as an accomplishment that could only be achieved by the elite among us, I now understand it to be, quite simply, the life each of us is meant to live. Finding your calling means placing less emphasis on what you should *do* and focusing, instead, on clearing a space inside from which your answers can emerge. It is in this place of stillness and strength that you will hear your inner voice, learn to trust it, and begin to act on its guidance.

Questions to Consider

- What personal challenges are you facing right now?

  ◻ Are any of them related to your desire for a more meaningful life?

  ◻ What are these challenges trying to show you or teach you? What is their message?

  ◻ How can you be more patient and compassionate with yourself as you move through them? Can you reach out for more support along the way?

Part I

Callings

Your Unique Path

Chapter 1

What Is a Calling?

If a calling is simply the life each of us is meant to live, then how do we understand what this means individually? For some, the term *calling* describes a career that one was born to do such as becoming an artist, a teacher, a doctor, or a priest. Since many of us haven't yet discovered our calling, is it possible to not have one? Do we have to muddle through our lives without the clarity and direction that a calling could bring? What about twentysomethings? During a decade full of confusion and uncertainty, is it even possible to find our authentic calling?

To explore these questions further, I asked numerous twentysomethings to give me their definition of the concept. Anna believes that a calling is "like a balloon you're firmly connected to. You aren't letting go of the balloon, and the balloon isn't letting go of you. You're being *pulled* toward each other. Over time, the cord gets shorter as you come together." On the other hand, Emma believes that a calling "sits between two extremes. On one end is the notion that you have complete control over your life, and on the other is the idea that everything is predestined and you have no control. A calling means that your choices do make a difference, but there's also a bigger plan operating at the same time." To Pat, a calling is "what drives you. It's what you want your life to be defined by at the end, when you're looking back."

At once deeply personal and widely universal, *calling* is a profound concept that means something different to everyone. In fact, some people even prefer to use other terms such as *purpose*, *path*, or *truth*. The first step toward finding your calling, therefore, is to contemplate its meaning for yourself.

This is particularly important for those of us in our twenties because we are making decisions at this age that will affect us for the rest of our lives. While navigating the endless choices and obstacles that lie before us, many of us struggle with the fear that we are failing to live up to our potential as well as with confusion about which direction to take. In the process we often feel like we just aren't *enough*. The irony is that even though we live in a world overwhelmingly connected by technology, it is common to struggle with a feeling of disconnection and loneliness.

The solution to such challenges is to develop your own sense of purpose. The way to accomplish this is to focus on the resources that lie deep within yourself. As long as you continue to search in the outer world for answers or approval, you will continue to feel lost. As long as you live without purpose, life will have an empty undertone. Once you have connected to your purpose, you will feel alive—even if you are not always one hundred percent happy or certain about your choices.

In the end, each of us must define success for ourselves. We must set the bar to meet our true desires and climb our own ladders. Only by doing so can we find our calling. Such a quest is well worth the effort because the rewards of self-discovery and authentic expression are great. As you awaken to your calling, you will also awaken to your *true self*, the free and full being who resides beneath your defenses, roles, and fears. Although this ride can be tumultuous at times, in the long run it brings satisfaction beyond anything you could experience while searching for happiness outside of yourself.

Essence and Form

At its core, I view *calling* as that which fuels you with meaning and purpose. Ultimately, it is your unique contribution to the world. I also believe that a calling consists of two fundamental aspects: essence and form. *Essence* denotes the fire you feel inside, while *form* denotes the tangible shape your calling takes in the world. Although many people think calling refers to a job, especially one associated with religious service, a job is just one form that it can take. Other forms include, but are not limited to, creative endeavors, hobbies, sports, outdoor activities, meaningful relationships, important causes, service projects, traveling, and children.

The form of a calling flows naturally from its essence. The essence of your calling may appear in your life as a higher ideal you are frequently preoccupied with such as love, service, personal growth, enlightenment, inspiration, peace, beauty, truth, joy, connection, creativity, knowledge, or social justice. If the essence of your calling is love, for example, you can express this quality no matter where you are or who you are with. Your calling already lives within you. As you develop and explore new areas of life, it will grow along with you.

Andrea, who became a high school French teacher at age twenty-eight, illustrates the difference between essence and form:

> The essence of my calling is to help young people, but that goes far beyond exposing my students to French language and culture. The core of what I strive to do is help the young people in my life realize their

potential, whether it's my students, my nephews, or others. I want them to understand how the choices they make impact themselves, their peers, and the world around them.

Andrea knows that even if she were to leave teaching, the essence of her calling would remain strong. She would find new avenues through which she could assist young people.

Contrary to popular fears, you cannot miss your calling. You may feel temporarily disconnected from yourself or confused about which direction to choose, but as you strip away the layers blocking your heart's desire, you will find the answers you seek. Because the essence of your calling unfolds in a spontaneous manner, try not to become overly attached to any one specific outcome. Over time, you will probably discover that your calling shows up in many different forms.

QUESTIONS TO CONSIDER

- What does the word *calling* mean to you?

- What do you think the *essence* of your calling might be? Consider the higher ideals you strive to live by and the larger causes that are most important to you.

- How does your sense of purpose (or lack thereof) affect the choices you are making today?

- What is holding you back and keeping you from expressing your purpose?

Living Your Truth

The path I am describing in this book is one that leads

to the discovery of your personal truth. Yet growth can be a messy process physically, mentally, emotionally, and financially. As you shift into greater harmony with yourself, you may find that certain elements of your life no longer work. Finding your calling means willingly embracing discomfort in order to let go of patterns (and sometimes people) that no longer serve your highest good. It also requires you to learn critical lessons, work through obstacles, and gain skills. During this time, life may bring different plans from the ones you had in mind, so try to stay flexible. These challenges are all part of the rewiring that occurs to prepare you to live at a higher, more fulfilling level.

Lacy, twenty-six, is a good example of a twentysomething who has faced the inner and outer challenges necessary to find her calling. "Everyone has a story," she says, "but it's what you do with your story that matters." Lacy's story did not begin easily. Born two months prematurely, she was rushed to surgery (the first of five over the next twenty years) when the doctors discovered she was missing an esophagus. For the first year-and-a-half of her life, Lacy ate through a feeding tube. The second surgery involved connecting her stomach to her throat so she could eat more normally; the third involved removing scar tissue that was causing her severe pain. The fourth, which occurred while she was in high school, was especially traumatic. The doctors performed a modified gastric bypass, which shrunk her stomach.

Throughout high school, Lacy experienced chronic pain. While the jagged scars along her neck and the left side of her chest clearly marked the sites of her physical pain, her emotional pain—although hidden—struck even deeper. Battling the sense that she was just not normal, Lacy struggled with depression, anxiety, and self-doubt. This led her to seek relief in therapy and an antidepressant for several years. Although antidepressants can benefit some people, for Lacy they were not entirely helpful. "In some ways it made me feel worse," she says. "I felt everything on the inside but couldn't express anything on the outside. I felt completely trapped."

Pain and suffering followed Lacy after she graduated from high school. Doctors told her that although she would never live a normal life, she could aim for a tolerable one. Lacy enrolled in classes at the local community college while holding various jobs and living at home with her parents. But she was constantly exhausted and had to drop out of school—a tremendous disappointment since neither of her parents had graduated from college and she was determined to do so. Fed up with the seemingly never-ending physical pain in her neck and chest, Lacy underwent a fifth and final surgery.

After surgery, while lying in yet another hospital bed, Lacy had an epiphany: she was *not* going to settle for a "tolerable" life. She would aim higher. "You're here for a reason," her inner voice spoke up, suddenly and resolutely. "Either you survive or you thrive. It's your choice. Focus on what makes your life *worth it*." Lacy realized that she had been allowing her low points to define her and decided to make some serious changes.

After initiating a discussion with her doctor, she began slowly decreasing her antidepressant until she was completely off of it. From there, she took several months to process her trauma by talking with family and friends, reading books that inspired her, and spending time alone to figure out who she was and how to make peace with herself. She constantly reminded herself of the choice she faced: *Either you survive or you thrive.* The line between the two, Lacy discovered, was dependent on her thoughts:

> I had been so frustrated, but I started realizing that life has taken great care of me. I'm still here, aren't

I? I focused on the good things that happened every day, like compliments people gave me and the activities I enjoyed, and the positive momentum just kept building. Once I owned my life, I wasn't ashamed anymore. I felt unique and purposeful.

Lacy's disciplined mind-over-matter approach contributed to dramatic physical improvements. "I was pain-free within two months, playing basketball and working out again. Now I only feel pain if I focus on it. I don't think about it 99.9 percent of the time, so I'm not in pain anymore."

Harnessing her renewed energy, Lacy made choices that stemmed from her true desires. "I decided it would be better to do what I really wanted rather than just going for the least scary thing I could tolerate." She transferred to an in-state university, moved into an apartment with two friends, and created her own major combining the classes she loved most: counseling, conflict resolution, and communications.

Since Lacy was on track to graduate later than her friends from high school, she paid close attention to how her peers fared after graduating. "The people who were successful had one thing in common," she says. "They networked. They established personal connections with people in fields they wanted to break into." Lacy gathered that "the best thing to do is talk to people. You win people over more than your college degree and résumé do."

To gain clarity about who she wanted to network with, Lacy followed a specific goal-setting process. She began to make lists that consisted of two columns: Gratitude and Goals. Under *Gratitude*, she would write down the things she felt most grateful for. Once in a positive frame of mind, she started looking for common themes. Lacy quickly noticed that she was especially happy when she connected with other people and when new opportunities came her way. Armed with this information, she began writing specific goals under the *Goals* column that she knew would make her happy.

The only requirements that Lacy set for herself were that 1) she was truly interested in achieving the goal, and 2) she believed it could be reasonably achieved within thirty days. Among others, her goals included meeting five new people in her evening class, attending a Toastmasters meeting, and connecting with a well-known national speaker. The very act of clarifying what she wanted and writing it down was powerful: time and again, Lacy's goals came to fruition within thirty days. Through this process, she also made connections that led to work as a corporate consultant and eventually she became a Certified Professional Coach.

In addition to her own determination, Lacy credits the supportive people around her with helping her pull out of darkness and create her best life. "My friends, my family, and especially my parents held the vision and believed in me even when I couldn't," she says. "I have never seen people love so unselfishly as my parents. So in those dark days I did it for them, knowing someday I'd be able to do it for myself. And I did, I have."

Today Lacy feels strongly that she is living her calling, and that her calling extends far beyond her job. "My calling is to be me so you can be you. From there we can propel forward together." She also feels that the more time we take to figure out who we are on the inside, the happier and more successful we will be:

> The twenties are a confusing and reflective time. You're expected to be everything, but you're inexperienced. You're thrown out into the world and society's telling you who you're supposed to be. But if you listen, there's this childlike voice saying, "Wait... don't you remember? *This* is who you are." Follow *that* voice.

As Lacy's story demonstrates, the path of following a calling is rarely smooth; each of us will face a unique set of challenges along the way. Because confusion and uncertainty are a natural part of growth, try to accept, rather than deny, these feelings as you move forward. In spite of the challenges, aligning with your own truth builds tangible confidence that can even be seen physically: it causes you to walk with your feet planted more firmly on the ground and your head lifted high. You breathe more deeply and act more calmly. If a calling is truly felt, you will be given everything you need for it to unfold in its perfect time and way. In the meantime, just keep breathing, gently direct your negative thoughts in a more positive direction, and continue to put one foot in front of the other.

GRATITUDE AND GOALS EXERCISE

If you feel confused about what you want, try the exercise that was so beneficial to Lacy. Perhaps it will help you find clarity, too.

Draw a line down the middle of a page. On one side, write *Gratitude*. On the other side, write *Goals*. Reflect on the people, things, and experiences you are most grateful for and write them down in the Gratitude column. Let inspiration guide you. The purpose of focusing on gratitude before goals is to tune into what you truly love in life first. This way you will not get bogged down in setting goals you think you "should" be interested in or "should" do, despite the nagging of your inner voice that they don't really excite you.

Next, look for themes among the items on your Gratitude list. Ask yourself, "How could these themes translate into tangible goals, even very simple ones, that could be achieved in the next thirty days?" Choose goals that naturally appeal to you, goals that are inspired by things you feel good about and enjoy in life. Write down one or two goals, then take action in the way that feels right for you.

Chapter 2

Hearing Your Inner Voice

The key to recognizing your calling is to pay attention to the way you feel. This means becoming acquainted with your wise inner voice. The inner voice is different from society's voice, the media's voice, or even from the voices of well-meaning family and friends. It knows what is best for you at any given time because it operates within the broader picture of your life in ways your rational mind cannot understand. In fact, the directives of your inner voice might not make sense to your logical mind or to other people around you. Yet it is through this internal guidance that you will receive unfailing counsel about whether to turn left, right, or go straight ahead.

To hear your inner voice consistently and trust in its direction, carve out some quiet time each day to connect with your thoughts and feelings—even if it is only for five minutes while you are cooking, exercising, driving, lying in bed, or taking a shower. Quiet time is critical in our twenties because we are bombarded with endless stimuli from the outside, ranging from the demands of our work and relationships to the vast amounts of information available through the Internet and other means of technology. If we aren't vigilant, these outer voices can drown out our inner guidance.

While I have chosen to use the term *inner voice* to refer to the intuitive self, you will not necessarily hear its messages like a literal voice. This wise part of your being communicates in countless ways, such as through intuitive hunches and desires, dream images (day dreams and night dreams), inspired thoughts, feelings of contentment and joy or of sadness and lethargy, irrational impulses, repeated urges to pursue something, uncanny synchronicities, or waking up in the night for no apparent reason. Its messages may also come through physical sensations such as gut feelings, butterflies in your stomach, a tight throat, goose bumps, or even a sudden headache.

In contrast to the wise inner voice, we each have a fearful inner voice operating as well. To uncover your calling, it is important to learn how to decipher the two. You can do this by paying close attention to your feelings. The wise voice makes you feel empowered. It uplifts you by nudging you toward the things you would love to do and reminding you of what you appreciate in life. It calms you down by centering you in the present moment and helping you find solutions to your problems. On the other hand, the fearful voice makes you feel tense. Instead of helping you solve problems and move forward, it constantly reminds you of past failures and defeats and warns you about everything that could go wrong in the future. It spins your thoughts in negative circles and can lead you to feel anxious, afraid, and paralyzed.

By tuning in to your feelings, you will be able to tell the difference between your wise voice and fearful voice. And once you understand how these two voices operate, you are free to choose which one you want to follow.

Following are numerous suggestions to help you hear

your wise inner voice more clearly. To help you process the ideas that are presented, I have included many questions and exercises. Reflect on them at your own pace.

Excitement and Passion

A calling brings with it an element of excitement and passion. If you pay attention, unexpected events may trigger these feelings within you. I know this to be true from my own life. One evening during my senior year in college, I drove to a bookstore with a friend to attend a lecture and book signing of an author I admire. As the author stepped up to the podium, a rush of energy surged through my body. Within minutes, I felt lightheaded, alert, and completely present. For the next hour, I was so high on excitement that I could hardly sit still. After my friend and I left the bookstore, I struggled to understand what had just happened to me. I was unaware that these sensations were pointing me toward my own calling to become an author.

Another clue came a few weeks after I graduated from college. My work in school complete, I loaded my belongings into my car and headed out of town, leaving behind the protective cocoon of my previous existence. As I glanced in the rearview mirror, I was suddenly gripped by the idea that I had to write a book. The essence of my calling—connecting deeply with others—had always been clear; the thrill I felt about the prospect of writing professionally told me that the next form my calling would take would be a book.

QUESTIONS TO CONSIDER

- Have you ever been gripped by an idea that you felt you *had* to pursue?

- What excites you, gives you energy, when you simply think about it?

- What makes your eyes, facial expressions, and hand gestures become animated whenever you talk about it?

- What do you talk about, read, or do for hours without getting bored?

- What do you do so naturally, what comes to you so easily, that you take it for granted?

Secret Projects and Dreams

Many twentysomethings have confided to me that they have a "secret project" they have either quietly begun to pursue or dream of pursuing. These ideas have such a grip on them that, on some level, they feel they can't *not* pursue them. Examples include moving to a new city or country, applying for an educational program, starting a business, making a film, building a website, becoming a professional musician, and traveling through a particular region of the world.

Often you do not get to choose your most cherished desires; they seem to choose you. They grab hold of your heart and nag at you over time until you agree to follow their lead. Early on, though, you may be reluctant to openly share these dreams with others. Now I understand that a calling is so important that it feels delicate and unsteady in the beginning phases. It takes a while before it is ready to move from the protected realm of essence into the exposed realm of form. If public exposure comes too early, it could leave you feeling weak and vulnerable. Before you are secure in your ability to achieve your goals, for example, you could become discouraged by others who tell you that they aren't realistic or practical. Or you might even be afraid that someone could snatch your ideas before they are fully developed.

Just like an embryo needs about nine months of shelter before it is ready for birth, your calling may need time to be safeguarded before you are ready to present it to the world. This time of gestation is important because it allows you to gain clarity and strength within yourself before accepting other people's input and opinions.

QUESTIONS TO CONSIDER

- Do you have a secret project or dream? Throughout the past few years, have you had a repeated urge to do something, go somewhere, meet someone, or take a particular risk?

  - How committed are you to achieving this goal physically, emotionally, and financially? What steps are you taking to move forward?

  - What stands in your way of pursuing your dream? Are you playing it safe in some way? Why?

  - What changes might occur in your life if you really committed to this project?

  - Evaluate your self-talk. Do you spend more time telling yourself why you can achieve this dream, or why you can't? How can you be more supportive toward yourself?

- Could you devote a small amount of time and resources to your dream on a regular basis in order to make it a reality?

Commitment and Drive

In the presence of a true calling, constant feelings of distraction disappear. You naturally want to see whatever you are doing through to its conclusion, and so you remain steadily committed to your path. Although it is normal to experience some doubt, uncertainty, and even fear along the way, you continually return to your core desire.

When Andrea entered massage school at age twenty-six, she knew that she had found her calling: learning about the human body and using this knowledge to help others. Unlike everything else she had tried in her twenties—including several different majors in college, many different jobs, and countless adventures throughout the United States and abroad—she did not feel restless when she was studying or practicing massage. Nor did she feel her customary urge to move on quickly to something else.

In fact, she was driven to learn more and to use massage as a launch pad for new professional endeavors. After school ended each day, Andrea went home and surfed the Internet for more information on the topics that had been discussed in class. Now she works in an acupuncture clinic by day and takes classes on various massage techniques at night. "I know I've found my calling because I'm always thirsty for more at the end of the day," she says. "There's no other fork in the road for me right now."

QUESTIONS TO CONSIDER

- When are you *not* distracted and restless? In other words, what are you doing when you are fully absorbed in the present moment?

- Think about a time when you felt completely committed to a project, cause, person, or hobby. How might this commitment point toward your calling?

Admiration, Envy, and Awe

Although the tendency to compare ourselves with others in our twenties can be frustrating, it actually has a positive benefit: admiration, envy, and awe can be one of the biggest indicators of a calling. Before you are ready to claim a personality characteristic for yourself, or follow a dream, you are likely to see it reflected in someone else. You might feel a pang of "Wow!" or "How did she do that?" A small voice may whisper, sometimes doubtfully, "I wonder if I could be like that, too?" You might even feel agitated in the presence of others who are pursuing dreams that are similar to your own, as if you are encountering something you are supposed to be doing yourself.

In psychology, the phenomenon of seeing traits in someone else that you do not yet own in yourself is called *projection*. Identifying projections is an extremely useful tool for finding your calling because each one acts as a benchmark that shows you the qualities you need to claim within yourself in order to move forward.

QUESTIONS TO CONSIDER

- When was the last time you felt admiration, envy, or even a touch of awe toward another person?

  - Can you identify the specific qualities this person possesses that made such an impact on you?

  - Is there any way in which you have been stifling these qualities within yourself?

> ☐ How could you begin to cultivate them in your own life?

- Take a moment to breathe deeply and relax into your body. Now imagine yourself as you would like to be, inhabiting some of the traits you admire in others.

> ☐ In this visualization, what are you doing?

> ☐ Is there anyone else around? If so, how do you interact with them and how do they relate to you?

> ☐ What do you look like? How are you dressed? How do you walk/talk/move?

> ☐ How do you feel inside?

> ☐ Does this "expanded you" have anything to teach you about your calling?

Childhood Nature

Your core nature as a child can also help you recognize a calling. Although you are not necessarily destined to step into the exact jobs you aspired to as a child, you can gain clarity about what will bring you fulfillment by reflecting on the activities that captivated you the most. Kate, twenty-six, says, "Everyone has something they're good at and positioned to do well at mentally, physically, and spiritually." She describes herself as having been "a creative, imaginative child" who loved making up stories, putting on plays and puppet shows, playing music, and singing. Even though she is now an adult, her essential nature remains the same. Her calling lies in the realm of poetry and storytelling, which she expresses through singing, songwriting, and playing musical instruments.

Questions to Consider

- Reflect on your core nature as a child.

    ¤ When were you the happiest?

    ¤ How did you most enjoy spending your time? What activities made time fly by?

    ¤ Did you prefer to be alone or with others? What type of people did you naturally gravitate to?

- If possible, find a picture of yourself "in your element" as a child. Study the photo closely and try to recall what you were feeling then. Ask yourself, "What can this contented child tell me about my calling?"

Life Review

To learn more about your purpose, Pat, twenty-seven, suggests that you pretend you are nearing the end of your life. "Look back and ask yourself," he says, "are there any options I would regret not doing or not experiencing?" Pat's ultimate goal is to make a difference in the lives of others. In order to have a maximum effect on others in the long run, he knows that he must focus on his own personal growth at this stage of his life. Every day he strives to become a better person through his close relationships and a better professional through the work he loves as an insurance underwriter. "Right now I'm challenging myself to broaden my horizons," he says. "My calling is to leave the world a more positive place, and I'll continue evaluating my choices over time."

QUESTIONS TO CONSIDER

- What are you most proud of personally and professionally?

- What do you want yourself, and your life, to be defined by in the long run? What would your ideal obituary say about you and the way you led your life?

- Are there any causes you feel compelled to help advance in your lifetime?

- Pretend that you are nearing the end of your life. What would you regret *not* having pursued or experienced? Allow these images to give you insight into your calling.

By working through these exercises, you may have uncovered some key patterns within yourself and the path you are meant to follow. By now, you probably have some sense of the essence of your calling. You may even realize that you have more than one. After all, your calling is dynamic, just like you are. If possible, express the essence of your calling in words.

One Step at a Time

Many twentysomethings want to see into the future before they are willing to act on their hunches. Before taking the first step forward, they sometimes want assurance that everything will come together "correctly" in the long run (e.g., they will be happy, financially stable, surrounded by friends, or in a positive intimate relationship). We are used to finding answers to our questions with the click of a button, so it is easy to understand why we may try to quell uncertainty and doubt by demanding that the future reveal itself before we try something new. But the result can be paralysis and an inability to make any decision at all.

In contrast, finding our calling involves reaching out to a new, and sometimes uncomfortable, way of thinking. It asks us to savor where we are right now and to give thanks for the positive elements of our daily lives instead of focusing on what is lacking. It also requires us to keep asking questions and listening for answers from inside without knowing how the "story ends." Fulfillment comes when we find ways to trust our instincts and live more fully in the present moment.

Sometimes you might yearn to be, do, or have something that currently seems out of reach or even impossible to attain. When this occurs, it is helpful to set an intention for your desire to manifest. You can do this by focusing on your desire, writing it down, and—if it feels right—sharing it with a trusted, supportive confidant. Also, consider *why* you want to achieve this particular goal: what positive feelings and benefits will it add to your life? All of these reflections set in motion the energy that will nurture your desire to fruition.

Next, relax and stay open to surprises. Remember that it's impossible to know in advance precisely how or when your intentions will unfold, especially since they usually do so in unexpected, mysterious ways. Instead of indulging in frustration that your desire has not yet come together, begin looking for evidence that it is unfolding: pay attention to the people who show up in your path, the unexpected opportunities you encounter, and the messages you receive through books, music, movies, and other sources.

After setting the intention for your calling to reveal itself, you will probably experience random impulses to take certain actions, sometimes odd ones. You can only experience the satisfaction that comes from living in harmony with your inner voice if you are willing to take the first step. Sometimes this can be as simple as calling a friend, going for a hike, or organizing a bedroom. At other times you might need to address larger challenges and make an appointment with a therapist, find a new job, deal with a relationship conflict, or tackle an addiction. What you do is not as important as taking actions that are true to your inner voice. And once you demonstrate enough trust to take the first step, the next one will be revealed.

Part 2

Work

What You're Called to Do

Chapter 3

Restlessness and Uncertainty

Many twentysomethings I know are in the midst of a work change—which can encompass changes in physical location and/or in education programs. And if they are not actually in the process of making a change, they are thinking about doing so. We are a restless bunch. Our hunger for more, our collective longing to manifest in the world the full potential of who we are, to share the gifts we are here to give, to not waste time, reveals itself as a near-constant state of transition. The rapid pace of change in our outer lives mirrors the rapid pace of change within.

Some twentysomethings who work full time are satisfied with their general line of work, but dissatisfied with their job's pay, benefits, or stress levels. They hope the next degree or promotion will resolve the situation. Others are flat-out unhappy at work and spend countless hours scanning the Internet for job postings. Unfortunately, after shutting off the computer, they often feel even more overwhelmed than when they logged on. Some twentysomethings piece together multiple part-time jobs while nurturing personal projects and hobbies on the side. Still others decide on additional education and anxiously apply to college or graduate school; enroll in professional training and certificate programs; or seek mentors through internships, volunteer work, or other settings.

Personal experience has shown me that the process of figuring out what we want to do with our lives is deeply personal and tugs at the core of our being. It is full of moments of clarity followed by days, weeks, months—even years—of confusion. The emotional toll of striving to find work you love, while coping with the work you have and taking care of the monthly bills, can be wearing. With so many choices, you might be painfully aware of all of the things you are *not* doing. You might struggle with self-doubt and wonder why you haven't "made it" yet. In the darkest moments, maybe you wonder if you ever will. Restlessness can lead you to question if something is wrong with you: *Why haven't I accomplished as much as other people? Will I ever figure out what I want to do? Why can't I just be happy?*

Chronic uncertainty can cause you to feel so overwhelmed that you become paralyzed. Or it can trigger you to make premature decisions in an attempt to establish security. It can also block you from believing in yourself enough to speak up on your own behalf in the workplace or from pursuing work that speaks more directly to your heart. You might move around laterally because it is safer than reaching for something higher, for something that truly inspires you.

RESTLESSNESS EXERCISE

If you feel restless in your current work situation but you are uncertain about what to do next, turn inward. If you don't know what you want to do, simply reflect on how you want to feel. For example, if you want to feel fulfilled but you do not, consider the following questions:

- What does being really fulfilled mean for you? What does it feel like inside?

- Where are you?

- What are you doing? How do you spend your time?

- Are you alone? Are others around you, and if so, who?

The key to this exercise is to challenge yourself not to get stuck in the loop of focusing on what makes you unhappy, because that will only make you feel worse. Go beyond it; take your imagination to the next level. Use what you don't want as a stepping stone to show you what you do want, and focus your attention there.

Over time, as you generate positive energy by focusing on how you want to feel, images will naturally emerge of what you want to do. You might even find that you do not need to make any immediate, external changes. Instead, you could discover a new way of thinking and being in the world that improves your current situation.

Driving Toward a Dream

The work you are called to do will probably not strike like a clap of lightning over your head. More often, it reveals itself through a series of impulses that occur over time. The key is to pay close attention to your feelings and then take action on each hunch in order for the next one to be revealed.

Brian, 28, found the work he is called to do by following his restless spirit. Growing up in a sports-crazed family in eastern Wisconsin, he loved playing baseball more than anything. He especially loved going to the ballpark with his dad. Although Brian played baseball avidly throughout childhood, he never reached the level of the pros. During his senior year of high school, he was faced with a tough choice: either attend a smaller college where he could join the baseball team, or accept an academic scholarship to the University of Minnesota where he would be unable to play the game he loved most. He chose the scholarship.

At the U of M, Brian played many intramural sports including basketball, softball, and football. But he longed to play baseball, which is "a deeply emotional game" for him. Eventually he approached the head coach of the U of M's baseball team and asked for the chance to be a walk-on. When the coach turned him down, Brian was heartbroken because his lifelong dream of playing in the major leagues was finally over.

Brian had no choice but to get on with his life, so he turned his focus on earning a business degree. He also began to dedicate the time he used to spend playing baseball to volunteering for Habitat for Humanity. Because of this detour into volunteer work, Brian discovered that he had another passion that ran as deep as baseball: helping other people. He loved feeling part of something greater than himself and knowing that he was making a difference for those in need. While still in college, he became president of the organization's local chapter.

Between his junior and senior years, Brian interned for a local bank. Upon graduation, this led to an offer of full time employment as a banker, which he accepted. For the next two-and-a-half years, he successfully climbed the corporate ladder. He even bought his own car and townhouse. But deep down he felt disconnected and lost. "Every day I was waiting for the day to be over and wondering when the rest of my life would happen," he says. "I didn't have an identity at the bank; it was out of sync with me as a person."

One day Brian came home from work and realized he

had to make a change. His mind began to wander back to countless "what if" conversations he had had with friends about how great it would be to work in the field of baseball. Unsure of where to begin, he got creative and decided to take action. Every evening for the next two weeks he prepared letters of application, accompanied by a résumé, to send to the general managers of all thirty major league baseball teams. He explained that although he currently worked for a bank, he had always had a passion for baseball, and he asked them for advice about how to break into the field.

Over the next few weeks, Brian received many discouraging form letters in reply. And then one day the telephone rang. It was Brian Cashman, general manager of the New York Yankees. Cashman had been so moved by Brian's letter that he had called in person to advise him to seek work in the minor leagues. Brian took Cashman's advice, researched teams on the Internet, and made some connections. He was soon offered an internship by the Los Angeles Dodgers at their spring training facility in Florida.

Undeterred by the necessity of taking a pay cut to follow his dream, Brian put in his notice at the bank, placed his townhouse on the market, and sold all of his furniture. Within two weeks he was on the road to Florida. "I was literally driving toward my dream," he says, full of excitement. "It was the most freeing experience! I didn't care if it worked out in the long run or not. It wasn't about success or failure. I was going for something that meant something to me."

After arriving in Florida, Brian soon realized that he would have to work long, ten-hour days to secure his internship and impress the higher-ups. As an additional part of his job, he was often asked to act as the mascot for a Dodgers' minor league team at night. Already worn out from a long day of work, Brian would dress up in the sweltering uniform for "Squeeze," a character with a grapefruit head, and run around rousing up crowds—all the while sweating profusely in the Florida heat. "I was willing to don the mascot uniform by night in order to get an amazing opportunity during the day," he says. "You have to be willing to do just about anything. Eventually someone will notice you."

And noticed he was: the LA Dodgers offered Brian a full time position at their spring training facility. For the next couple of years he worked in a position that he describes as "helping the Dodgers be the best they can be, from the business end of the game." Although he still missed playing baseball, Brian loved his work because he was always surrounded by the game. "Even when I'm just looking at a budget spread-sheet, it's meaningful to me because it's related to baseball."

Eventually, however, the Dodgers decided to close down their spring training facility in Florida and open another one out-of-state. Brian was given notice that in a couple of months, through no fault of his own, he would be out of a job. Although he could apply down the road to work at the new facility, there was no guarantee that he would be re-hired. "I didn't want to just sit around and wait and hope," he says. So once again he took action.

One day, while browsing job postings online, Brian came across an opening for a coordinator position with the Office of the Commissioner of Baseball. Thrilled by the job prospect, he quickly sent off an application. Soon thereafter he was called for an interview, and eventually he was offered a six-month contract. Although his new job would be located in New York City, Brian did not hesitate to accept it. "I can just pick up and go in my twenties," he says. "In my thirties and forties, once I have a family, it won't be realistic."

Today Brian is in transition, preparing for his move to New York. By taking risks and following his instincts, he feels that he is living his calling:

Calling means something different for everyone. For me, it's about living out your goals and dreams with no regrets. Then you don't think later on, "Should I have done this?" or "Could I have done that?" Tomorrow, next week, next year . . . those are just excuses. Today is the best day to start chasing your dreams.

In order to chase our dreams, Brian encourages us to concentrate on believing in ourselves:

It's a tough road if you don't believe in yourself because people will tell you that your dreams are impossible. But if you do believe in yourself, a hundred people might tell you that you can't do something and just one person might tell you that you can. And you'll hear that one person louder than all the rest.

Although Brian is deeply satisfied with his career choices, he emphasizes that "every day is not a walk in the park." Due to the demands of working in baseball, he has limited personal time and his future is uncertain. "If you really want to do something you enjoy, there'll be some sacrifices," he says. "I work tons of hours and the pay's not great, but I'm passionate about baseball. I like taking home something more than a paycheck. When you follow your dreams it won't be all rainbows and butterflies, but it'll be worth it."

Ultimately, Brian would like to become the general manager of a baseball team or work in collegiate sports as an athletic director. He shares his thoughts on facing the unknown:

Don't interpret restlessness and uncertainty as a negative thing. It forces you to put in the time and effort to make something good happen, instead of waiting for change to come to you. Losing my job with the Dodgers could have been seen as a negative thing. But it forced me to keep my eyes open and I found a new, great opportunity—one that's even better for me in the long run. Once again, I'm driving into the unknown. It's exciting and nerve-wracking, but I can't wait.

When to Stay and When to Go

As Brian has learned, restlessness has a positive purpose: it can lead to rewarding work if you are willing to trust your instincts and go with the flow of your life. To find work you love, you do not necessarily have to pack up all of your belongings and move across the country. But you do have to pay close attention to your life and listen to the guidance of your inner voice.

When you relax, it becomes clear that you are led into detours for a reason. Like Brian, you might even lose your job only to discover something better down the road. And if you do not have your dream job right now, it does not mean your current work is unimportant. You may be developing the interpersonal, practical, and emotional skills that will later be essential to succeed in the job of your dreams.

When restlessness strikes, sometimes the best option is to begin planning an exit strategy and looking for a new job. At other times, it's better to stay put for a while longer. If you constantly jump ship at the first sign of discontent, you might never experience the fulfillment that comes through developing new skills, building solid relationships, and contributing to a larger cause. You could also become frustrated by the demands of adjusting to new tasks and end up feeling like you are failing to achieve anything at all.

But if you feel persistently dissatisfied with your job, your inner voice is trying to communicate with you. Perhaps it is urging you to address a problem in the workplace that you have been avoiding. Or it might be nudging you to move in a new direction altogether. To decipher your next step, take some time to grow quiet, tune into your heart, and ask that the truth of your situation reveal itself. Your inner voice won't lie. Instead of quitting, do you need to confront an uncomfortable issue? Do you need to adjust your expectations and make a greater effort to adapt to your current situation? Or is it time to move on to a new environment in order to achieve maximum personal and professional growth?

If something is really bothering you at work, be sure to take responsibility for your own part in the problem and the solution. You can do this by specifying what is bothering you, considering various options for improving the situation, and then—if it feels appropriate—initiating a conversation with the person who can help enact a change. If you don't speak up for yourself, who will? When you are clear about your values and needs, accept your truth, and then speak it out loud, you might be surprised at how people and circumstances line up to support you. On the other hand, you might find that speaking up does not lead to positive change. When this occurs, it is time to seriously consider leaving your job and moving on to something else.

If you have pressing financial circumstances, you may need to temporarily remain in a job you dislike while seeking new work. During the transition period it is important to take action toward a new job, perhaps by researching new companies, sending out résumés, and networking with people who work in fields you are drawn to. It is also important to draw on your inner resources to create work you love. For example, you could spend a few minutes each day reflecting or writing in a journal about how you want to feel in your next job. You could also develop a vision of the working environment that would make you happiest, including the type of people you want to be surrounded by and the income level that best serves your needs and desires. During this time, ask yourself what qualities and skills you need to develop in order to become highly attractive to new employers or clients. Or just set an intention to find work you love and then see what happens. All of these actions prepare you for the work you are called to do.

Embracing Restlessness

Work is a powerful catalyst for personal growth. It all begins with the process of asking yourself what you want to do with your life. But you don't have to figure it all out in your twenties. Few of us do. It is through the exploration, the confusion, and the restlessness that you will learn about who you are and what contributions you are here to make. Although restlessness can be uncomfortable, it is a sign that you are expanding beyond your previous limitations and paving the way for the next phase of your life and career.

Erin, a thirty-three-year-old artist, bookstore employee, and marketing consultant has learned that feeling restless does not automatically mean something is wrong. She believes that restlessness is a natural, creative impulse, an avenue through which our inner voice communicates with us. Erin reflects on her winding journey through her twenties and thirties:

> I've been constantly struggling with "what should I do for a living," thinking it was just one thing. Well, I know now that I want my career and work to be an ever-changing, fluid kind of venture. I want to go where I'm taken and give back in many areas, not just one.

Because your calling emanates from within and is not restricted to any one job, person, or thing, your inner voice may lead you, as Erin's did, into many different areas. Even if you feel that your twenties have been full of random experiences that do not amount to one significant achievement, every experience is valuable because it has helped shape the person you are today.

It is perfectly normal to dabble in various jobs and/or educational programs to learn what type of work, colleagues, pace of activity, and environment best suits you. Finding work you love can even be a process of elimination, of trying different things to learn more about what you do—and don't—want. For example, you might not know that you prefer to work on a team until you have completed several independent projects. Or until you work in a highly structured position, you might not know that you actually perform better when given a great deal of creative freedom.

The truth is, some degree of restlessness surrounding work is normal. The notion that you can plan an entire career in your twenties is a myth. You can certainly take important steps toward your goals, but just when you think you have figured out where you're going, a new crop of doubts might pop up! An element of uncertainty surrounding your career can actually be a good thing. Uncertainty gives rise to new possibilities, and these new possibilities could reap far greater rewards than your tightly held plans ever would have. As you transition through different stages of your life and personal development, you might find yourself led into numerous lines of work.

The first step toward finding and creating work you love, therefore, is to embrace the restlessness and uncertainty you feel inside. Instead of fighting these feelings or distracting yourself from them, try to make peace with them. How do you do that? By feeling their energy in your body, breathing into them, and then weighing all of your options so that you make the best decisions you can today. When you make peace with your emotions and express gratitude for the positive aspects of your life, you also grow into the person you need to be to handle the bigger and better things that are coming.

Transferable Skills Exercise

Even though you might feel restless in your current work situation, you are probably developing transferable skills that will help you in the future. Transferable skills are those skills that are essential in many different lines of work including problem solving, customer service, information technology, research, writing, planning, management, leadership, and communications.

When you acknowledge the transferable skills you are building, you are able to appreciate your current job more fully. With this in mind, take a moment to view your current job as preparation for the work you are called to do. (If you are unemployed or in school, reflect on what you have learned from past jobs.) You are likely gaining transferable skills that will be necessary to get hired or start a business in the field you are drawn to, and to succeed and thrive in that field as well.

- What transferable skills are you honing right now? Are you becoming a clearer communicator? More practical? Better at time management? A more effective leader?

- How are you growing personally? Are you developing assertiveness, self-esteem, or emotional intelligence?

- If you do not enjoy your work, let your imagination wander into the type of work you would love to do.

▢ If you could do anything with your days, how would you spend your time?

▢ How could the skills and experiences you are gaining now help you build a successful career in a related field in the future?

• If you feel stuck because you are learning very little from your current job, but you don't know what type of work you truly want to do, consider the following questions:

▢ What kind of skills are you using when you are the most content? Do the hours disappear when you are using your hands to build a piece of furniture? When you are listening to your friends' problems and helping to counsel them? When you are caring for children? When you are advocating for someone who is being treated unfairly? These are all clues to your calling. If you listen to your heart, if you pay attention to the times when you feel the happiest and most fulfilled, you will discover clues that will point you in the right direction. And sometimes the best approach is to just pick something you're curious about and see where it leads you. After all, you can always reevaluate your choices over time.

Chapter 4

Meaningful Pursuits

During our twenties, we yearn to discover what makes us unique so we know how to make an authentic and enduring mark on the world. Even if we work primarily to bring home a paycheck, I believe the majority of us also want to feel a sense of meaning and purpose in our job. Meaningful work gives us the sense that our time, energy, and actions *matter*. It gives us an avenue to connect with something larger than ourselves and to make a difference in the lives of others.

Through personal experience and hundreds of conversations with others, I have observed that meaningful work grows out of who we are. It engages our strengths, reflects our values, allows us to express our individuality, and contributes to a cause we deem important. It also takes place within an environment and at a pace in which we feel "at home." If you are introverted by nature, you have plenty of time to work alone so you do not become drained; if you are extroverted, you frequently collaborate with others to keep your spirits up.

You know you are engaged in the work you are called to do when you feel satisfied while you are working, and also when you are thinking about work. Family, friends, or the media may not agree with your definition of meaningful work. In fact, a job that fulfills you could repel someone else, and vice versa. Even if your daily tasks appear to be dull or mundane to others, you might find value in your work if you help other people, if you enjoy the company of your coworkers, or if the job fills a particular need you have at this stage of your life. Similarly, others could have a career that appears to be exciting or important, but if you went down the same road, it might not be fulfilling.

To find work you love, take the time to define success for yourself. Stay true to your own calling instead of trying to emulate someone else's. If you do something because you feel like you "should" do it, but you lack genuine enthusiasm about it, your intuition is trying to lead you in another direction. No one else can quantify the worth of your work; you will only know its value by the satisfaction you feel inside. Emma, twenty-three, summarizes this point using the metaphor of clothing: "Sometimes you wear clothes that other people say look good on you, but they just don't feel right. Even if something looks nice, that doesn't mean it fits."

Creating Meaningful Work

You are always growing into the person you need to be to do the work you are called to do. Because meaningful work grows out of who you are, creating it requires a continued focus on self-discovery. But if your schedule is so packed that you have little time to reflect on your life, it might be difficult to know what you truly want—much less create it. Some people would love to find meaningful work but harbor a number of reasons why they believe they cannot do so, such as constraining financial or personal circumstances. While these concerns may be valid, they should not be used as an excuse to do nothing at all. You can always prioritize a "time-out," even if only for a few minutes a day, to reconnect with your deepest longings and brainstorm new ideas.

In my experience, the process of creating meaningful work involves three major elements: 1) clarifying your values, 2) connecting with others who share your values, and 3) setting and meeting small, manageable goals that move you toward your dreams.

Clarifying values

Your *values* are the principles that reside at the core of who you are. They define what you "stand for" and point to the type of work that will fulfill you over time. Your values reveal themselves in your favorite ways to spend free time such as getting together with family and friends, immersing in nature, spending time with animals, giving back to the community, helping people solve their problems, creating works of art, being politically active, playing sports, or traveling. They are also apparent in the human qualities you hold in high regard such as integrity, intelligence, empathy, assertiveness, peacefulness, sense of humor, or dedication to service. You can also gain insight about your values by reflecting on the bigger causes that matter the most to you.

Not only do your values help you clarify the type of work you want to pursue, they also point to the lifestyle that will, and won't, make you happy in the long run. For example, becoming a park ranger will lead to a significantly different lifestyle from working in an office, owning a restaurant, teaching history, driving a truck, becoming a scuba diving instructor, going to nursing school, or earning a living as a musician. If your top priority is spending time with family and friends, you might quickly burn out in a profession that requires you to take on a great deal of overtime. If you love being outdoors, you could become depressed sitting at a desk all day. If your main goal is to buy a house and support your family, you may feel increasingly frustrated if you barely earn the minimum wage. If you yearn to be "on the go," you will probably chafe in a slow-paced setting.

To find work that matches your natural rhythms, try not to give too much weight to job *titles*. Although certain titles might sound appealing or glamorous, it is the reality of the day-to-day pace and activities, as well as your income, that will determine much of your satisfaction at work. Instead of focusing solely on job titles, be sure to also look for work that supports the lifestyle you want to lead and incorporates job duties you enjoy.

Connecting with others

Once you have begun to clarify your values, and how they relate to your professional life, focus on expanding your network of people who share them. This could be as simple as sending an e-mail to a few people whose line of work intrigues you. You could request a twenty-minute phone conversation to ask questions about how they reached this stage of their career, the elements of their work they like and dislike, and any advice they may have for you. Many people are flattered when others show sincere interest in their work, and they enjoy sharing their experiences. Plus, there is always the possibility that someone will unexpectedly help launch you into a new, rewarding chapter of your life. If you don't reach out, though, you'll never know.

Setting and meeting goals

As you continue to focus on self-discovery and connect with others who share your values, a vision will naturally begin to emerge of the career you want to develop. Sometimes this vision is large and sweeping. At other times it is quite narrow; you might even feel as if you are holding a flashlight with a weak battery and can only see a few inches in front of you. Either way, follow your hunches and set small, manageable goals that can be reasonably achieved within a few days, weeks, or months—and then take action to meet them. If you set goals that are too far-reaching, you might feel too overwhelmed to move forward at all. Simultaneously, pay attention to any sabotaging thoughts and behaviors you engage in and begin replacing them with new habits that serve your growth. By setting and meeting smaller benchmarks that serve your larger vision, you will grow in self-confidence and set the stage for success.

QUESTIONS TO CONSIDER

- Aside from earning money, what is your primary motivation for working? Personal growth? Creative development? Making a difference in society? Expanding your social and professional network? More power and influence?

- Consider your current work. How meaningful is it to you, personally?

  - How do you typically feel when you are getting ready for work, and getting home from it? Fulfilled? Drained?

  - If you derive little meaning from your work, what internal and external blocks are holding you back from pursuing work you love? Are you making any excuses that keep you stuck?

  - What is one small goal you can achieve this week to begin creating meaningful work? Consider researching a company that intrigues you, e-mailing someone who works in a field you are curious about, or saying no to a request you do not really want to accept so you have more time to pursue a project you enjoy. After you decide on your goal, write it down and commit to following through.

Personal Mission

Gita, thirty, believes that "Your calling is your personal mission. It's the statement you make to the world about who you are." Reflecting on her core values, she says, "My calling is community-based service. I want to contribute to society so even people who don't feel normal can succeed." Gita's calling of community-based service can be traced to her heritage. During the 1960s, her father arrived in the United States from India for the first time. When he stepped off the plane in the Rocky Mountain West, with only a small amount of money in his pocket, he was dismayed to realize that something was going terribly wrong with his hair. Before he had left India, he had styled it using coconut oil as a gel. Now, in freezing winter temperatures, his hair was literally beginning to crack!

Although Gita's father encountered many cultural differences in the United States, both small and large, he did not let any of them stand in his way of making a good life for himself and his family. Through hard work and education, he was able to bring his wife (Gita's mother), his siblings, and many extended family members to the United States. The family settled in California, where Gita was born.

While Gita was growing up, her home was always packed. Her father prided himself on bringing people together and extending generosity in the community. Aunts, uncles, friends, and neighbors abounded, with little children constantly underfoot. Community was Gita's bedrock. She loved living in a house filled with people, partaking in her family's Hindu rituals, and making friends with people from many different cultural and socioeconomic backgrounds. She also prided herself on volunteer and service work.

As a teenager, Gita loved to paint and dreamed of becoming a social justice artist. However, she eventually chose to pursue the more practical field of social work and completed both her bachelor's and master's degrees by the time she was twenty-six. Throughout her studies, Gita's passions focused on two areas: improving the welfare of children and counseling others. "Counseling is very spiritual," Gita says. "It's about finding yourself and creating balance."

After graduate school, Gita applied for social work positions all over California, but was unable to find work due to statewide budget cuts. "For eight months I was living with my parents and getting depressed." To lift her spirits, Gita reached out to what she knew best: community service. She traveled out-of-state to help with a weeklong service project geared toward empowering young people. She loved the program and became very involved in it. She also made connections that led to a job offer at a local therapeutic preschool. The position was perfectly aligned with her passions for counseling and protecting children.

Gita gladly accepted the job, and she still works there today. Her duties include helping struggling parents improve their parenting skills, supervising others who work in the program, and doing administrative work. In addition to her job, she volunteers for a county commission that focuses on early childhood development, serves on the board of an independent bookstore, and facilitates diversity trainings in her community. All of these projects fuel Gita's mission of community-based service and allow her to collaborate with people who share her values. She views each endeavor as an important part of the work she is called to do, whether or not she is being paid.

Gita's major challenge is bridging the gap between her Indian heritage and the American culture in which she lives and works. She struggles to explain her education and work to her relatives. "Counseling is a very Western concept," she says. "It's hard to explain what I do to the Indian community. They don't understand why you wouldn't just go to a regular doctor for your problems. When I talk about therapy, they wonder if I'm talking about physical therapy."

Despite her challenges, Gita is energized by her work because it makes a positive impact on her community. But this does not mean that she will always work at the same job. Her ultimate goal is to collaborate with like-minded people to open a community center that serves low-income and/ or traumatized women and children. It would also provide counseling services for individuals and couples. Contemplating her future, Gita says, "I'm always transitioning, always trying to find myself. We're always growing."

One way to recognize meaningful work is that we suddenly have almost limitless amounts of energy. When we are in this zone, when we are engaged in projects that mean the most to us, a timeless quality takes over and we often feel like we're not working at all. This is true for Gita; in return, rewarding opportunities continually arise for her. She encourages twentysomethings to "Put yourself out there and try to believe in yourself. You'd be surprised by who wants to listen to you and learn from you."

Making a Contribution

Like Gita, many of us find that meaningful work involves making a contribution to society. Your contribution could occur in a direct, personal way, perhaps by helping others overcome a particular struggle you have faced. Or it could occur more subtly such as through your kind words to customers, the compliments you pay your coworkers, the decorations you put up to create a beautiful workspace, or the silent, supportive thoughts you choose to think about the people around you. Work instantly takes on a deeper dimension when we focus on making a positive difference in our environment.

Amy, twenty-eight, knows that when we show up fully at work, we help the people around us and express our purpose no matter what we are doing. As a manager at an insurance company, Amy's mission in life is not to process insurance claims. It runs deeper than that. "My calling," she says, "is to help people develop as individuals. I do that every day as a manager, which is really important to me." Amy is happy with her work because she dedicates herself to creating a sense of community in the office and to the growth of the people around her. In turn, she continues to be promoted to positions of greater responsibility, which she loves. She also earns a good salary that affords her two of her greatest pleasures in life: the ability to travel and own her own home.

Whether you work at a large corporation, in the nonprofit sector, or somewhere else entirely, every moment presents an opportunity to be of service in some way. And even if your job is "just a job" that you do not find particularly meaningful, you can still make the best of each day by bringing your full self to work and spreading positive energy into your environment. This does not mean, however, that you should neglect yourself by constantly saying yes even when you would rather say no or by working to the point of burn-out. After all, your greatest contribution arises when you stay connected to your true self. Sometimes the only thing you need to do to be a positive influence is adjust your mindset. You can always steer your thoughts in a loving direction, look at a difficult situation from someone else's point of view, or communicate your truth more compassionately.

In the end, we will only get as much out of our work as we put into it. When we show up fully for the people around us, the rewards come back to us multiplied.

QUESTIONS TO CONSIDER

- What is your personal mission statement? When answering this question, consider your own definition of success as well as your most important core values.

- Reflect on your unique talents and skills, those you have demonstrated since childhood or have developed due to life circumstances. If you have trouble identifying these abilities, start by paying attention to what you are doing when you feel most alive, the times you make a positive difference in other people's lives, and the compliments you repeatedly receive.

  ¤ How could you apply your gifts to influence society?

Chapter 5

The Creative Instinct

For some twentysomethings, the most meaningful career is a creative one. For the purpose of this chapter, I will use the term *creative career* to refer to a hobby or interest that becomes a livelihood. Although some people are not interested in making a living from their hobbies, others feel so much passion in a particular area that they will be dissatisfied long-term if they do not at least try. Even if they work as a server in a restaurant, for example, they might *really* identify as a musician, a photographer, or an entrepreneur. Deep down, some of us long to inhabit our creative selves so fully that there is no distinction between our daily activities and the projects that mean the most to us.

Whether or not society labels you as an "artist," creativity is an essential part of your calling because it is the wellspring from which your true self arises. Creativity gives birth to your unique visions, passions, and perspectives. We are all creative beings. We can't *not* create. Some people express their creativity through artistic pursuits such as dancing, painting, sculpting, acting, writing, choreographing, or playing music. Others prefer domestic pursuits such as entertaining friends and family, raising children, gardening, cooking, doing crafts, making clothes, or building and fixing household items.

Still others are more technically inclined and enjoy designing websites, developing software programs, and inventing new products. Not everyone expresses their creativity overtly, though. Some people express themselves more subtly, perhaps through their sense of humor, the way they accessorize their clothes, or their innate ability to connect with other people.

When given room to flourish, creativity reveals new—often surprising—insights about yourself and the world around you. It calls forth the best you have to offer. But when you stifle your creativity, you may be haunted by the sense that something is missing in your life. Over time, you could even grow numb or depressed due to lack of spontaneous self-expression.

If you want to earn a living from your creative talents, start by considering the path that compels you most strongly, even though this could change over time. For example, you might long to collaborate with others in an organization that excites you. Or you might hold a more independent vision and dream of starting your own business. Often the best place to start is to seek mentorship and community in a field that interests you. You could apply for internships or educational programs, start volunteering, join a club, or attend a workshop. Through these activities you will make contacts, develop skills, and gain information that helps you determine where to go next.

In my own life, the process of becoming an author has been a balancing act. It has included working at various jobs while negotiating work schedules that allow me the time and space I need to write, research, reflect, and put my creative work into the world. My experiences in the workplace have allowed me to gain practical skills, make new friends, and stay financially afloat while moving forward with my creative dreams. Similarly, if you decide to develop a creative career, you will need to find ways to pay your bills while also taking practical steps to launch your new venture. This will help you grow as a person and move steadily toward your goals without prematurely placing pressure on the new endeavor to support you financially. Once you get serious about bringing your dreams to fruition, the task is to carve out a balanced schedule so you cover your creative and financial bases.

Healing Internal Blocks

As you consider what role you want creativity to play in your life, take some time to look within and unearth any lingering creative blocks. If you do not shed light on them, they could become a sabotaging force. Common blocks to creativity include an assortment of fears, such as fear of failure, change, criticism, the unknown, revealing a buried truth, or going broke. At the core, many of us just don't believe in ourselves. Often this pain has past roots. Perhaps a classmate insulted your artwork, a teacher shamed your best efforts at writing a story, or your parents dismissed your desire to act in community plays. As a result of early influences, you might have gotten the message that your creative work is unworthy of being taken seriously.

On the flip side, you might also be wary of growing beyond your previous limits and attaining new heights. Success can trigger fears of disrupting key relationships, igniting jealousy or resentment from others, changing familiar routines, and managing additional responsibility.

Working through fears

Whatever your fears may be, there are several steps you can take to reclaim your creativity. Start by identifying the internal blocks that are holding you back and letting your fears "speak": What is preventing you from expressing yourself creatively? Is there anything you are afraid of? As you begin this process, take note if there are painful memories or traumas lingering within you. If there are, consider seeking professional help from a therapist or support group. Otherwise you may want to write in a journal about your fears and anxieties, or talk them through with a supportive friend or family member.

You can also relieve your fears by talking or writing out your "worst case scenario." The purpose of this exercise is not to focus excessively on negative scenarios; rather, it is to look at your fears objectively and rationally so you can place them in the broader context of who you are today. This exercise can also help you develop the confidence that comes from knowing you are strong enough to handle whatever comes your way, and to formulate strategies to move in the direction of what you do want. As you unearth your fears and give them breathing space—while also seeking support from others when you need it—eventually they will no longer hold the power to control you from behind the scenes.

Dreaming without limits

Second, allow your imagination to run wild. Let yourself dream without limits. Often the best time to do this is immediately upon waking up in the morning. Many people find that their days are full of details and errands that drain them. When you focus first thing in the morning on a higher purpose and the things that make you happy, you launch an intention that influences the entire day. This intention guides you to spend your time wisely, perhaps by stepping outside of your normal routine and trying something new, or by saying yes to the things you really want to do and no to those you do not.

Nurturing creative projects

Next, as you connect with your heart's longing, carve out a supportive space in which you can nurture the creative projects that mean the most to you. Maybe you would love to design greeting cards, grow a garden, take up a new sport, paint a picture, plan a party, learn to play the guitar, build a website, cook a special meal, write a collection of poems, or invent a product. You can get started by gathering together the supplies you need. Then schedule a bit of time each day, week, or month to indulge your creativity. This could mean signing up for an evening class or just closing your door to interruptions for thirty minutes a week. Approach this time with a childlike attitude; you could even view it as "playtime."

Because it is normal to be especially vulnerable to criticism during the beginning phases of an endeavor, pay attention to your self-talk and the feedback you invite from others while you are getting started. If, early on, you demand perfection from yourself or receive stinging criticism from others, you might feel too discouraged to keep going.

Also, remember that you don't need to approach these projects with the end goal of making money or turning them into a career. People choose their work for widely different reasons, and your career path might take you in a different direction altogether. Many people enjoy cultivating their creativity for the intrinsic benefits of doing so such as pleasure, growth, emotional expression, meeting new people, and a heightened sense of well-being that spreads into every area of life. And when you live authentically, you can express your creativity in many different work environments, just by being yourself.

Looking for open doors

Finally, as you reignite your creativity, look for the doors that open and propel you forward. When you pay attention, you will encounter support in unlikely places. You might receive random compliments from others, come across encouraging passages in songs or books, discover the perfect workshop being offered in your community, or receive unexpected invitations. When you walk through the doors that open naturally, instead of pushing hard against those that don't want to budge, you could find yourself stepping onto a path that takes you even farther than you imagined.

Your Name Lives On

Erik, thirty, discovered what he wanted to do as a career by diving into his favorite hobbies. As a jewelry maker and martial arts instructor, he requires a hands-on approach to work. "If I can't put my hands on something, it's like it doesn't exist to me," he says. "I'd feel like I'd accomplished nothing if I sat in an office all day."

Erik grew up in a tiny rural town on the East Coast with a population of about fifteen, before moving to the West Coast with his father and brother when he was in seventh grade. Erik's father, who was a toolmaker, owned a machine shop while Erik was growing up. "I grew up with machines and metal all over the place," he says fondly. "I also loved martial arts; I took lessons and watched all the Kung Fu movies." Like his father, Erik developed an interest in making tools and decided to learn how to make knives. While he was still in high school, he bought books on knife-making, along with the requisite tools and materials, and proudly made two of them. Soon thereafter he signed up for a weekend seminar with an expert knife and jewelry maker.

During the seminar, the instructor told Erik about a local arts and crafts college. Erik felt the tug to follow in his father's footsteps and become a tool machinist, which his father would have loved, but his creative instincts won out. "Even though I have a technical and analytical side, my creative side has always been stronger," he says. "I wanted a more creative career than my dad's."

Erik enrolled in the arts and crafts college, but soon fell behind. He finally dropped out completely after having taken just a few courses. "I was so frustrated because my technical abilities weren't advanced enough to create the things I envisioned artistically." As a result, his self-esteem faltered and he "partied too much." During this time, Erik's brother introduced him to a local jeweler who was starting his own business and needed help around the shop. Erik jumped at the chance to work for this man and be mentored one-on-one.

"From the outside it might look better to get a college degree," he says, "but you have to decide for yourself what's really better for you. Maybe I didn't stay in school, but I immediately began making connections and developing my skills." Erik's circle of connections grew to the point that he was offered a job by a well-known local jeweler who owned a family business. Erik became so skilled that he was promoted to lead jeweler while he was only in his mid-twenties.

"I gained a really good reputation, even though I was oblivious to it," he says. "I just focused on making customers happy through the jewelry I made for them." With his broad range of experience, Erik became a self-described "jack-of-all-trades":

There are so many specialties in jewelry, but I like working with lots of different people because you learn so many different processes. My specialty is stone carving but I enjoy other things like wax carving, hand engraving, and fabricating jewelry. I also love the precision and detail of laser welding.

After working for the family business throughout much of his twenties, restlessness for something new kicked in. "I felt like I'd learned all I could and wanted to move on," he says. Erik had become keenly interested in antique jewelry and hoped to gain more experience with it. He mentioned his desire for a new job to friends and acquaintances. Soon, a jeweler specializing in antique repair and restoration approached him with an offer to work in his store. Erik still works there today.

Erik values the artistic element of jewelry making the most, but he also acknowledges that a broad range of skills is the foundation that allows him to be truly creative:

> Once you've got the basic skills down, you can use your imagination. The more you know, the more creative you can be because you aren't limited to one specific skill set. Now, sometimes I make jewelry that leaves me in disbelief—it's so original it doesn't even seem like it came from me. I like making customers happy, but fulfillment comes when I create something truly unique. That's art.

Erik's career has been marked by the theme of teaching and mentoring, beginning when he dropped out of school in favor of being mentored one-on-one. At first he was the one being mentored. Now he mentors others. He consistently helps new apprentices learn how to improve their jewelry-making skills and, as a side endeavor, he also teaches at a local martial arts studio. "Part of what makes work meaningful is mentoring others," he says. "When I have a lot of knowledge in an area, I feel like I have to share it. It seems to come naturally to me."

Erik believes that the creative impulse resides in human nature. "Part of art is realizing that the things you create will be around after you're gone. It would be so cool to have someone dig up a ring one hundred years from now and see my name on it. Your name lives on that way."

Focus and Persistence

As Erik knows, turning a hobby into a career means staying focused on your inner vision and being persistent in your efforts to follow it. You can do this by patiently developing your skill set, increasing your knowledge about the field you want to enter, building a professional network, and finding supportive mentors and friends who encourage you and help mold your abilities. Above all, it is important to take your own potential seriously, even when it's tempting to doubt and criticize yourself. Building a creative career is like tending a garden. Without consistent care and the right conditions, a garden will not bloom. Even when times get tough, you owe it to yourself to chip away at your dreams because this nourishes the soil in which something beautiful will grow.

I have observed that the people who are most fulfilled with their work are those who stay attuned to their feelings, and then take risks and follow their hunches. Regardless of the type of career they pursue, they accept that it will take time for their goals to come to fruition. Even when it appears that nothing is happening, they stay true to the calling they feel inside. They do not spend a great deal of time mentally ruminating, seeking approval from others, or repeating thoughts and behaviors that are not making them happy. Once their inner voice urges them to do something, they get in motion and act on it.

When you say yes to your calling, your life will change from the inside out. You will experience joys and challenges you could not foresee. Because change can be unsettling, it's natural to feel ambivalent before moving forward. But when you connect to the creative spirit that lives within you, you gain the courage to take action on your dreams because you know that you aren't defined by success or failure. You also learn that what you perceive as failure right now could actually be a great gift when you turn it around and look at it in a different light. Instead, you are defined by an intangible, unwavering presence inside of you that remains strong no matter what the outcome may be.

Questions to Consider

Like Erik, many twentysomethings prefer creative work as diverse as floral design, musical pursuits, acting, farming, or building things. Does this sound like you?

- If so, what creative outlets do you enjoy the most?

- Even if your current job is not particularly "creative," do you carve out time in your schedule to expand and express your own vision? How does your mood shift when you take this time for yourself? What holds you back from doing so?

- How much support do you receive from the people in your life for your creative endeavors?

- Does anyone criticize or diminish your efforts in a way that is not helpful? If so, how can you stop inviting this person's feedback?

To cultivate your creativity, start small by honoring your creative instincts and making time for the projects that are meaningful to you. Consider giving yourself just thirty minutes or one hour a week. Be consistent, and over time this simple practice could even lead into full time work you love. If you would like more support, or just more people with whom you can share your work and give and receive feedback, it can also be incredibly rewarding to seek out a mentor, an organization, or a community that shares similar interests.

Chapter 6

Financial Abundance

While we navigate through the challenges of a decade filled with infinite possibility and with fear that we will make the wrong choices and fail to achieve our dreams, one of the central issues we must face is our relationship with money. When it comes to following our dreams, money can either free us or bind us. This is why it is critical to clearly understand the role it plays in our lives.

Our relationship with money spans a broad spectrum. Some of us find work we love that satisfies our deepest needs and pays well, too. Others struggle just to survive. Some lack adequate health insurance or have none at all, and feel overwhelmed by the need to pay off multiple debts while taking care of monthly bills. Others embark on a lucrative career and jump on the fast track of raises, bonuses, and promotions. For some people, this track is deeply rewarding; for others, it's not. It depends on whether or not we are following a path that is true to our heart's desire.

Why do we display such a wide range regarding our ability to find work we love that also pays well? Certainly economic factors play a role, including the state of the economy, the amount of financial assistance we have—or have not— received from our family, and health insurance policies set by forces beyond our control. Yet beneath these external circumstances lies an additional factor: money is not just a physical currency, but also a flow of energy, of giving and receiving.

Blocks in your beliefs can lead to blocks in the flow of abundance into your life and cause you to cap the amount of money you allow yourself to have. The beliefs you acquired during childhood are particularly powerful. For example, your parents might have showed you that you can make a decent living following your calling as long as you are persistent. Conversely, they might have showed you that it's hopeless to take your dreams seriously because you will never be able to support yourself or your family if you do. Or you might have had an experience that made you feel as if you aren't worthy or talented enough to succeed and that you would fail if you tried. Or maybe you started to experience success only to have been met with demands, jealousy, or estrangement from relatives or friends. One lesson you could learn from this is that success is painful and separates you from those you love. If living at a survival level makes you feel comfortable, you might become very good at giving, but struggle to receive. You might also fail to educate yourself about finance management and spend or invest money unwisely.

Shifting Your Attitude

The principle that money is a flow of energy comes with a corollary: human beings are connected to a flow of energy, too. This means we have a magnetic quality that amplifies whatever we focus on most strongly. If you focus on what is going wrong, you are likely to experience more negativity. If you focus on what is going right, you are likely to attract more positive feelings, circumstances, and people into your life. By focusing on what brings you joy, you can create a life you love more quickly and with less stress. Shifting your thoughts in a positive direction helps you feel lighter, more relaxed, and more empowered. It ignites a spark of inspiration that flows through you and guides your actions. When you radiate the enthusiasm that comes from following your curiosities and passions, you draw supportive people and synchronistic events into your life that help nurture your goals to fruition. You are also more likely to put in the time and effort necessary to succeed than when you follow a path that doesn't inspire you.

A second important principle is that words have power. For example, if you tell your family and friends, "I'm going to become a professional singer even though I don't know yet how it'll happen," your words will encourage them to believe in and support you. They may go out of their way to give you advice or make contacts for you with people they know. As a result, you will begin to experience unexpected opportunities that help sew together your dreams. On the other hand, if you tell your family and friends, "I'd like to be a professional singer, but I know I could never make a living at it," they will probably believe this too, thereby reinforcing your negative beliefs and experiences.

A third important principle is that money makes up just one part of the concept of *abundance*. True abundance develops from appreciation for all of the wonderful people and things in your life—right now, at this present moment in time. In other words, it involves gratitude. When you choose to feel grateful for what you have, including the amount of money you already have, you naturally attract more to be grateful for. You also shift into a state of mind and heart that allows you to receive the good things coming your way. On the other end, focusing on what is lacking in your life disempowers you and perpetuates a negative cycle. Which would you rather feel? The choice is yours to make.

QUESTIONS TO CONSIDER

To find work that feeds your true self, and to thrive in this career, take some time to identify your core beliefs about money. After all, these beliefs dictate many of our actions and set us on a course of financial abundance or lack. They lie at such a fundamental level of ourselves that we will not be able to change our experiences until we become conscious of what they are and begin transforming them.

- What does money mean to you? What feelings and images does it evoke?

- How educated are you about finance management?

  - Do you follow a written budget? Do you read books and articles about money, listen to the advice of financial experts, or meet with a financial adviser? Are you paying off your debts and spending, saving, and investing wisely?

  - Is there an area of your personal finances to which you need to pay closer attention? What simple, practical actions could you take to begin turning this area around?

- Think about your current work situation.

  - What are its biggest rewards? Biggest drawbacks? On a scale of one to ten, how content are you?

  - What role does money, or your fears about it, play in the type of work you are pursuing?

- Reflect on your childhood.

  ¤ What kind of an example did your parents, friends, and community set about money and financial security? How do you think this could be influencing the choices you are making today?

- Over the years, have you accumulated any limiting beliefs about money?

  ¤ If so, start by identifying these beliefs. Then become aware of the words you repeat over and over to yourself as well as the words you speak out loud to others. Are they positive and affirming? Or are they negative and denigrating? When you catch yourself spiraling down a negative cycle, try to gently shift your thoughts, words, and actions in a more positive direction.

Basking in Greatness

Melody, twenty-six, applied these principles to create her own successful business. She grew up in a small, rural town in a loving family that did not have much money, and she was driven and ambitious from a young age. She watched her mother work hard to obtain a college degree while her father supported the family. "Once my mom graduated and started working," she says, "I knew we had more money because suddenly the food got better."

Melody graduated from high school early and then spent eight years in college, working full time to pay for her undergraduate degree. During this time she also met her husband, Aaron, and gave birth to their daughter, Jenna. In addition, she and Aaron bought their first home. Before doing so, they met with a financial planner. This turned out to be a life-changing experience for Melody. "It was amazing to learn about investing and how money grows over time. You can really make your money work for you!"

After graduating from college with a degree in finance, Melody observed a void in the education system when it came to teaching young people about money. She felt a strong desire to use her skills to fill this void, so she decided to found her own nonprofit organization. "I looked for the job I wanted and didn't find it, so I created it myself."

Today Melody uses her passion to teach middle and high school students how to make smart decisions with their money. The mission of her business is to deliver personal financial literacy programs to young people. The curriculum focuses on four key areas: banking, credit, savings, and investing. The entrepreneurial spirit thrives in Melody's family. Her husband also started his own business in real estate investing, which has evolved into home remodeling.

As a small business owner, Melody is particularly mindful of the power of her words and demeanor when she speaks about her work to her family, board members, and volunteers. She understands that words can help us become financially abundant or hinder the process. She also looks for evidence that her goals are already beginning to come together and then shares her success freely. With a daughter to support and two businesses to help run, Melody knows that she needs more than practical savvy to help her family become financially abundant, so she focuses on positive thinking:

> For anyone who's an entrepreneur, positive thinking is absolutely imperative! There's a lot of stress and problems that arise from starting a new business. But if you dwell on these problems, you'll find that they just get worse because you're putting out your negative thoughts and feelings, and that's what will

be drawn back to you. I've been immersing myself in positive thinking lately and have seen some amazing results. I also converted my husband, the skeptic, and he's also finding good results.

Because Melody offers her educational services for free, she is dependent on fundraising, grants, sponsorships, and donations for income. To help generate the money her business needs to thrive, she applies the following positive-thinking techniques:

I have a bulletin board where I post things that I want, inspirational messages, and things I like about my life. I'm working on visualizing that I already have everything I want. This has been kind of hard for me, but I've been reading some books that have really helped. I also meditate and do yoga. I look at the bright side of things and really try to think the best of everyone. I proceed with things as if I already have them—this scares my husband and board of directors sometimes!

Earlier this year Melody's business ran out of money, which meant that she was unable to pay herself a salary. Instead of panicking, she applied her positive-thinking techniques, projected confidence, and set the tone for success:

I continually reported to my board that even though the funds were low, I felt great about the organization and knew things would turn around. We did have an amazing turnaround. We taught a record number of students; we got a ten thousand dollar donation; and I got appointed to a state task force. After that I began to think about our upcoming fundraising event and how wonderful it would be to have our state treasurer speak. It was a very optimistic wish, but someone introduced me to a director in his office who made it happen.

Melody has concluded that her persistence and attitude play a large role in the success or failure of her business. "I used to get so grumpy every time I'd pay the bills," she says, "but now I just go with it because I know things will turn around. I firmly believe that both my husband's business and my own are wonderful and will be highly successful, so that's what I focus on." To maintain a peaceful frame of mind, she consistently reminds herself of everything she appreciates about her life:

Even during hard times, our life is incredibly wonderful. We have a great relationship and a wonderful daughter. We enjoy life and do pretty much everything we want. Why wallow in worry when I can bask in the greatness of our lives?

Ultimately, Melody's focus on gratitude and positive thinking serves a larger purpose: contributing to young people's lives through education. She loves the work she has created and is gratified by the enthusiasm of her students. "They love learning about money," she says, smiling. "It's empowering for them. They know these skills will help them reach their dreams."

As Melody's story demonstrates, it is essential to educate ourselves about finances during our twenties. This is especially true because many of us did not receive much—or any—training in this area while we were growing up. It is also important to remember that the quality of our thoughts either helps or hinders our ability to receive the financial support we need to achieve our goals. Our feelings tell us whether we are on the right path (through joy) or wrong path (through discontent), and the positive words we speak enable those around us to share in and help create our vision.

As you shift your limiting beliefs, give thanks for the good you are experiencing right now, and focus on the positive experiences you want to have in the future, you will become more magnetic to people and opportunities, naturally connecting to a flowing cycle of abundance. And as you become more abundant in your own life, you will have more to offer the world.

Abundance Exercise

To create greater abundance in your life, try the exercise Melody described. Buy a bulletin board and post different items on it such as photos, articles, and symbols that express what your heart most longs for. Choose images that remind you of experiences you want to have, personality traits you wish to develop, things you want to create, messages of personal and financial success, and elements of your life that you love and appreciate.

Hang this board in a place where you will see it often. Allow it to remind you of the good things that are just around the corner. Then pay close attention to your daily life and expect to see evidence of positive results. The more you look for these results, the more you will experience them.

Part 3

Adventure

When You're Called to Explore

Chapter 7

New Possibilities

A calling challenges us to grow into our full human potential, and adventure plays a central role in the process. At heart, adventure is a new experience of ourselves in the world. Usually precipitated by an urge to step outside of our comfort zone, adventure stands as the doorway between the person we perceive ourselves to be and the person we yearn to become. It's vital to discovering our purpose because it thrusts us beyond automatic patterns into an expanded set of possibilities for our lives.

Feeling stuck in a rut or confused about what you want is a sign that it's time to step out of your familiar routine for a little bit so you can view your life from a new perspective. Whether you take a year, a week, or just an afternoon, spending time in a new environment can provide the space you need to discover yourself in a new way. The type of adventure you choose is not the central issue. Instead, the key is following the hunches that tug at you most strongly, for they are trying to lead you to your calling. Anything that beckons to you strongly does so because it resonates with who you are today and who you are becoming tomorrow.

When you open to new possibilities, you might find yourself being led into unknown terrain without a sense of where you are headed or how this detour fits into the larger picture of your life. You might be challenged to face your fears, and change aspects of your daily life that feel safe and comfortable but are actually holding you back. Even if it is not readily apparent, periods of wandering can be the perfect remedy for helping you determine who you are and what you want. Over time, they can redirect you to a far more satisfying path.

Irrational Impulses

For better or worse, uncertainty is a close companion to most twentysomethings. Unrelenting doubt about the future can be unsettling, especially when you are trying to make critical decisions about where you belong and what you want to do with your life. To ward off uncertainty's lingering presence, we sometimes map out timelines that makes us feel secure. We set dates by which we want to achieve the major benchmarks in our lives such as entering—and succeeding in—a career, finding a life partner, and having children.

While timelines can help you move steadily toward your goals, they can also create even greater internal stress. The notion that you can plan your entire life in the midst of such an unpredictable decade is an illusion, and illusions tend to die hard. Timelines are often unrealistic expectations in disguise; failing to meet them can lead to self-disappointment and depression. If you look closely at the benchmarks you have put in place, you may find that they do not actually ring true to your heart. In reality, they may have been set in motion years ago by someone else, such as a parent or teacher. Or you may have adopted life goals based on society's standard measures of success, before taking the time to consider what you really want.

But your inner voice operates in present time only. Even

while carrying out carefully crafted plans, maintaining a flexible attitude is essential for personal happiness. If you stay open to the unfolding of your own path, life may ask you to change course when you least expect it.

Kelly, twenty-six, constantly tried to map out her life in her early twenties. She eventually realized, however, that this approach was causing her more suffering than satisfaction. "I had lots of plans, but they didn't work out the way I thought."

Kelly grew up in Colorado and chose to stay close to home after high school. As an undergraduate in college, she settled on a double major. She chose the first one (economics) to appease her practical instincts and the second one (creative writing) to fulfill her passion. As each year of college passed, Kelly pondered more deeply the career path she wanted to pursue after graduation. Her reasonable, practical side identified an interest in health, so she decided to become a health care administrator. She wrapped up her senior year by writing her economics thesis on health care reform.

While Kelly had many positive experiences during college, anxiety and depression constantly simmered underneath her upbeat demeanor and led her to seek support from a school counselor. Graduation was a happy occasion, but it did not quell her emotional unease. To the contrary, she felt suffocated and ached for a change of pace. She eventually decided to move to Wisconsin and live with her aunt.

Upon arriving in Wisconsin, Kelly secured temp work to sustain herself while she applied for full time jobs in the health care field. Despite the fact that she was applying for jobs that perfectly fit her long-term career goals, Kelly couldn't muster any genuine enthusiasm for any of them. "These were all jobs

I *thought* I wanted," she says, "but I'd look at the descriptions and hesitate, thinking 'I don't know...' Even my own mom thought my business suit looked awkward on me!"

Kelly's rut was suddenly interrupted one day when an intriguing e-mail landed in her inbox. Her aunt had forwarded a message from a program coordinator who was seeking a native English speaker to live with Buddhist nuns in Nepal and teach them English. Kelly's gut instinct responded forcefully. She thought, "That's the coolest thing I've ever heard of!" She paid close attention to this enthusiastic reaction, for it stood in stark contrast to the malaise in which she had been mired.

Not wasting a minute, Kelly shot off a reply noting her interest in the position. "If I get this," she told herself, "I'm going." When she received an offer to join the team, her practical side was nowhere in sight. "I decided to go without even consciously realizing it." In hindsight, she understands that a deeper part of herself was guiding her to embark on this new adventure.

Although she was thrilled by her impending adventure, Kelly grew hesitant in the days leading up to her departure. The reality of her hasty actions began to sink in. She was not going through a formal program, and she had only heard about this opportunity through a distant friend-of-a-friend-of-a-friend. She was taking a big risk based on little more than a gut instinct. Would she be safe? Was this all a big mistake? As the plane soared away from U.S. soil, Kelly worked hard to resist fears ranging from nervousness to panic.

Even after arriving in Nepal, she continued to experience high levels of stress. This is a natural part of stepping into the unknown, and it actually triggered positive results. "I was so out of my element that I was extra aware of everything happening around me," she says. "The stress enhanced my experience." Luckily, Kelly quickly relaxed once she arrived at her new home in the nunnery. Her twelve fun-loving house-mates put her immediately at ease with their affection and good humor. Spanning a broad range of ages, each nun wore a bright maroon robe and had a shaved head.

As Kelly settled in and her stress levels subsided, she came to adore the nuns and view them as close friends:

> The nuns were really loving. I could tell how much they cared about me because they'd hug me all the time. Even though I always helped with the chores, they took me in as an honored guest from day one. Their sense of reality was so different from mine, but there were a lot of similarities too, like love and a hysterical sense of humor.

Despite the language barrier, the nuns incorporated Kelly into their daily routine as much as possible. She especially enjoyed teaching them informal English lessons and sharing tea and meals. Outside the house was a garden where the nuns grew their own vegetables and spices for meals. To honor their Hindu neighbors, they did not eat meat. And because they strove to live pure, respectful lives, they abstained from alcohol. Many of the staple foods Kelly had grown accustomed to in the United States were not available, especially sweets. She didn't realize how much she missed them until the day the nuns shared a rare treat with her—cookies—and she gobbled them up so quickly that she later felt guilty.

The nuns devoted their lives to piety above all else, and they prayed for over four hours daily. "Their purpose is to pray and keep higher consciousness alive," Kelly says. "They're living this life for their whole society." The prayer routine included a two-hour morning and evening *puja*, which Kelly describes as a boisterous song-meditation routine involving chanting, horns, drums, and cymbals.

"At first the puja was so loud that it hurt my ears," she laughs, "but over time I grew to think it was beautiful." Although the nuns were sad at times, they generally seemed to be very content and much more relaxed than Americans. Their devotion to their faith inspired Kelly to become more dedicated to her own spiritual growth.

To Kelly's dismay, a government coup erupted in Nepal about one month into her stay and the phone lines and Internet were cut off. In the middle of the turmoil, the King of Nepal reinstated the Internet for a brief period of time, and Kelly rushed to check her e-mail. She had received numerous concerned messages from her family urging her to come home as soon as possible. Although she was heartbroken by the prospect of cutting her time short and leaving her cherished new friends, Kelly succumbed to her own fears and the fears of her family and decided to leave.

During the taxi ride to the airport, regret and sadness raged through her. And then—in an instant—a powerful, reassuring calmness descended on her. It spread throughout her body and mind and left in its wake an unfamiliar, unwavering sense of peace. In that moment she was convinced that the decision to leave was out of her hands. Kelly describes this sensation as one of "no power" during which her self-centeredness melted away and she was carried along by a force larger than herself. This state of surrender was the polar opposite of her previous tendency to try to plan everything in advance. To Kelly's surprise, it offered her tremendous comfort:

> I tend to carry the weight of the world on my shoulders. I think Americans feel like we can do whatever we put our minds to if we're strong and powerful enough. Sometimes that's true, but for once in my life I had a strong sense of something bigger than me being in charge.

Still she concedes that "Coming home was really hard. I still think about the nuns all the time."

Kelly returned to the United States with a new perspective on life that allowed her to uncover her true calling: writing. She became aware that she is the least distracted when she writes, and when she is not writing, she is always thinking about something to write. She also realized that she felt strong pangs of envy when she heard about people her age who were successful writers. It dawned on her that this was a message that she wanted to become a writer, too.

Kelly decided to accept a position at a small publishing company in Chicago. This work was closer to her heart's desire than health care administration had been, but she soon grew unhappy again. Even though she was working in a field related to writing, she was still resisting her calling to become a writer herself. "I was playing it safe," she says.

Today Kelly is interning at a magazine in Colorado, and she practices inhabiting her greatest dream of working for *National Geographic* by telling others about it whenever the opportunity arises. Through the ups and downs of her twenties, she has learned to value painful emotions as well as positive ones because she has discovered that all emotions communicate important messages. Persistent feelings of anxiety, depression, and confusion speak to us through the discomfort we feel in our bodies. They tug at us until we excavate and transform whatever aspect of our lives is out of harmony with our true selves.

Kelly's emotional pain serves as a signpost to her genuine desires. It teaches her to appreciate how precious life is and how adamantly she wants to use her time wisely. "I can't handle doing things that are wrong for me," she says. "My struggles help me accelerate. They're a huge physical push to pay more attention to myself." Kelly sums up how her adventure in Nepal helped her find her calling:

Going to Nepal turned my being upside down. It made me stand back and look at my life, and it shook me up a lot. I know my gut better now. Following it is the right thing to do. Health care was a distraction from what I really want. Now my path leads to writing. I can't *not* write. I'm good at other things, but I can't emotionally do anything else for the rest of my life. A calling means pursuing your passion and what you truly love. We need to respond to our calling, not try to understand it all the time.

To twentysomethings who are in a rut or who are trying to figure out where to go or what to do next, Kelly shares what she has learned:

The impulses that make no rational sense are the ones you should follow the most. Be brave and don't shy away from something because you're scared. You're better off facing it. If you have strong feelings inside, maybe you know more about what you want than you realize. Other people might be right in a lot of ways, but you have to be your own biggest advocate.

While Kelly did everything "right" (i.e., going to college, choosing a sensible career path, searching for a good job), she longed for new possibilities and greater meaning in her life. Like Kelly, many of us also harbor such longings. If we stuff them down for too long, we are likely to descend into numbness, unhappiness, or depression. But if we heed their messages and follow them, they can transform our lives. This is why it's wise to pay attention to impulses that, at first glance, seem to be illogical because they do not match your preconceived plans and timelines. They are often overt clues pointing to the heart of your calling.

Whenever you step outside of your comfort zone, you gain a new perspective on your life, your values, and how well your day-to-day activities match up with the stirrings of your life purpose. Although a new adventure will not solve every problem you face, especially if there are deeper emotional issues that need to be addressed, it will teach you to be more self-reliant. Such times can bring great doubt and periods of struggle, but they are never in vain. In the future, when you are looking back, you will probably see that you were learning the exact lessons you needed to learn in order to grow.

QUESTIONS TO CONSIDER

- Define adventure for yourself. What does it mean to you?

  - How does adventure show up in your life? In what areas are you already living adventurously?

- Have you ever dropped everything to follow a gut instinct? (In responding to this question, don't concentrate on dramatic events alone. Think about small things as well, such as the time you took the afternoon off work to go on a short road trip.)

  - If so, what benefits did you gain from this experience?

  - How did these benefits influence your mindset and day-to-day life?

- Do you currently feel an impulse to do something that makes no rational sense?

    □ What might happen if you took just one step toward this impulse?

    □ What would that step be?

Chapter 8

Risks and Rewards

In our twenties, the rewards of adventure are great. Examples include becoming more confident and self-reliant, increasing happiness and fulfillment, broadening our worldview, forming new friendships, and even discovering unexpected career opportunities. To reap its tremendous rewards, adventure challenges us to take some risks. But there is a direct link between our self-esteem and the ability to do so. If you are ruled by your fears or a constant need for security, you will probably place conditions on the messages of your inner voice. You will only hear what you want to hear: the impulses that don't shake up your self-image, career, relationships, or finances too much.

To overcome this confusion, remember that the key element in any adventure is not what you do; it is the energy with which you do it. Part of finding your calling is cultivating an adventurous spirit. This means a willingness to acknowledge all of the whispers of your inner voice, not only those that guarantee comfort and stability. Of course, you do not have to immediately drop everything to chase every elusive hunch, but you do need to give yourself time to dream about the stirrings in your heart, for they are there for a reason. Because the inner voice typically presents you with only one snippet of information at a time, and not a crystal ball with long-term answers and assurances, be prepared to enter new terrain from time to time.

An adventurous spirit does not require eradicating your fears, only that you identify them and move forward with self-awareness. It's normal for your deepest fears to get stirred up whenever you are getting ready to leave behind one phase of life and enter a new one. You might be afraid that others will disapprove of your actions or judge you harshly, that you will fail or run out of money, or that you will be alone. Instead of avoiding your fears or trying to drown them out, focus on softening your perspective and loosening your defenses.

How do you do this? Simply by observing the rise and fall of your fears, by becoming curious about their origins, and by developing compassion for the way they fiercely try to protect you. Whenever you feel afraid, return to your breath and the simplicity of this moment. Fears are often triggered by thoughts about the past and future; each breath reminds you that they hold no real power over you right here and right now. As you gently support yourself through your fears, you will develop the strength needed to pursue the adventures that are uniquely right for you.

Beyond Your Bounds

Nick, twenty-seven, understands firsthand the risks and rewards surrounding adventure, for he craves it so intensely that he cannot contain it or compartmentalize it from other areas of his life. Growing up in a small Midwestern town with his parents and older brother, Nick was a self-described "flighty, scatterbrained kid." He hated being indoors, preferring instead to spend time on his parents' hobby farm, where he was surrounded by the family's sheep, horses, ducks, and chickens. And he loved the long summer days spent fishing, biking, playing baseball, and running through the forest with his friends.

After Nick graduated from high school, curiosity and a need for money spurred him to apply for a summer job as a firefighter with the Department of Natural Resources. The department trained him to recognize weather patterns, read maps and compasses, use tools, and understand fire. His first assignment was putting out small fires across his state. It was not until later in the summer that he encountered his first major catastrophe: a huge fire raging in the Nevada desert.

The trip changed Nick's life. "Every day was amazing," he says. "It was constant adventure. I loved every minute, even sleeping outside in the desert. But I did worry about rattlesnakes crawling into bed with me and finding scorpions in my boots."

At the end of the summer, Nick went back to the life he had planned: going to college to earn a degree in physical education and health. But his gregarious nature could not be restrained and he was more interested in having fun than in succeeding academically. His grades plummeted so low that he decided to transfer to a community college closer to home, hoping for better luck the second time around. But even in his new environment, Nick struggled to stay on track. This time fishing was the culprit. "If I'd studied as hard as I fished, I'd have done really well in school."

Nick finally decided to quit college for good. At first he felt like a failure. As time passed, though, he realized that he had made the best choice and that college was not the right outlet for his abundant energy. The summer before he quit school altogether, Nick worked for a company in California that fought fires where urban and wilderness areas intersected. His job was to identify endangered houses and try to save them whenever possible by pulling away flammable materials and installing sprinklers on rooftops. Although Nick was happy to have the job, he found the work tedious. His attention frequently drifted instead toward the Sierra Hotshots, the firefighting crew that battled the toughest fires. "I wanted to be with those Hotshot dudes taking care of business," he says.

Nick returned to California the next summer with the intention of working his way up to Hotshot. He and another young man named Shane were hired as sawyers, which are crew members who cut away trees and branches. As a result of the long hours spent together in intense physical labor, Nick and Shane soon became best friends. This helped Nick realize that one of the main reasons he was so drawn to firefighting was the spirit of camaraderie that developed among crew members:

> You have to get along and trust each other because the nature of the work is so dangerous. Everyone looks out for everyone else around them. When you're willing to sacrifice for each other, you develop a bond really quickly. I love that hard-working camaraderie, being with a team of very close friends. We literally trust each other with our lives.

Nick and Shane worked extremely hard that summer, as well as the next one, always striving to perform their work impeccably and without complaint. Even so, they were not promoted to Hotshot. Disappointed, they made a pact with each other that if they didn't achieve their goal by the end of the following summer, they were done. But to their happiness and relief, both men were offered positions with the Sierra Hotshots the next year. Nick was ecstatic. He could hardly believe he had landed his dream job alongside his best friend. The pair packed up and headed for the foothills of the Sierra Nevada Mountains to begin training with their new team.

It soon became obvious to Nick that he had joined an extremely tough, professional outfit. The Hotshots focused intently on their work and strictly enforced a "No Whining Policy"—even in the face of sixteen-hour days, extreme weather ranging from heat to snow, broken fingers, poison oak, and high altitudes that caused them to vomit. While crew members offered each other unwavering support in times of need, they also recognized that the nature of their work was so grueling that if whining were permitted, it could easily become the norm and overrun their real task at hand: protecting the lives and property of citizens.

Nick has now spent two years as a member of the Hotshots. "Deep down we all know we have one of the toughest crews in the nation," he says. During the winter months he takes time off to heal his body, let his mind unwind, and catch up on quality time with family and friends. During the summer months he often works in the wilderness fourteen consecutive days, sixteen hours a day, before taking a mandatory two-day break. On a typical workday, he and his crew wake up around five o'clock in the morning, devour packaged dried foods for breakfast, then hike back to the perimeter of the fire they were fighting the day before. At night the crew sleeps on the ground inside the fire, which means in an area that has already burned.

While Nick loves the sensation of adrenaline coursing through his veins, the rush of adventure he experiences as a firefighter is not his greatest reward. Knowing that he is making a difference in the lives of others is.

The greatest reward is saving countless lives and houses. When there's a huge fire coming at a city, and you're just a bunch of little humans who beat this super force of nature—well, that's unthinkable to most people. We're a team of very strong, very determined people, and we don't fight fires for the money. We do it because it needs to be done. We run on pride.

Yet Nick also admits that there are drawbacks to his thrilling career. For starters, he routinely misses out on the summer activities he loves. In addition, it is difficult to maintain an intimate relationship due to a schedule that requires him to be away for long stretches at a time. Still, Nick stays focused. "This is purposeful work," he says. "Even when it's tough, we just tilt forward and keep going."

For Nick, a calling develops naturally from a series of questions that we routinely ask ourselves: *What am I meant to do in this life? What makes me happy? What gets me through the day?* The answers to these questions grow and change over time. He reflects:

> For me, it's fire. Generally I don't have a lot to say on other topics, but fire makes me tick. It gets in your blood. The best days of my life are two weeks in, covered in dirt, finally beating a fire. It's an unmatched feeling. Fire gives me the rush I'm looking for in life: constant adventure, excellent physical condition, great friends, and a sense of accomplishment.

While Nick is adventurous by nature, he is not without fear. "It can be scary being in a dangerous position," he says, "but you learn your capabilities." When we feel fear, he advises us to "just do it" because, he says, "The longer you wait to conquer a fear, the more you're going to be scared of it. The only way through is to take action, and it gets so much easier every time you do."

Nick has his sights set on an even more adventurous goal in the future: becoming a smokejumper. This is a wildland firefighter who parachutes into remote areas to combat forest fires. Nick intends to fight fires for as long as he can. He also realizes that the desire for a family may propel him into city firefighting down the road so he can maintain a more regular schedule.

In reviewing the ups and downs of his twenties, Nick concludes that periods of confusion are ultimately valuable because these are the times that push us to make tough, important decisions and to grow exponentially:

If you're unhappy, start new. You need to go out on your own to become the person you want to be. Then when you come back, you'll feel great. You lose control to get it back. You can't be ashamed of yourself for leaving home and building yourself up. Surround yourself with great people and you can make yourself into who you want to be in a short period of time. Adventure is pushing yourself beyond your bounds and coming out safely on the other side. You just have to trust that you'll come through it.

Like Nick, we all hunger for adventure, even if we work in an office every day. Understandably, not everyone wants to turn their favorite adventures into a career, preferring to keep the categories of "fun" and "work" separate. But whether the desire for adventure is relatively minor or intense and all-encompassing, everyone feels its pull to some degree.

To experience the growth that adventure brings, be prepared to try new things and take some risks when your intuition nudges you to do so. Such risks are well worth it because they help lead you to the life that is distinctly right for you. Along the way, asking why you are here helps you dig beneath your personal concerns and tap into the inner reservoir where your greatest talents, passions, and skills reside. When your priorities are clear, you can enter the unknown with greater confidence and ease.

QUESTIONS TO CONSIDER

- Reflect on the struggles you have experienced in your twenties.

    ◻ In hindsight, were any of them triggered because you were trying to follow a path that was not right for you?

    ◻ How did these struggles redirect you to a new, better path? What were the rewards of changing course?

- Are there any adventures you have been longing to pursue?

    ◻ What is holding you back from moving forward? Are any fears keeping you from taking action in some area of your life?

If you want to try something new, but you are reluctant to drop everything to pursue it, brainstorm ways you could start on a smaller scale. For example, if you want to live abroad one day, start researching the area of the world that intrigues you. Read books about this region, watch movies that are filmed there, talk to immigrants, eat in restaurants that serve food that is typical of the culture, and begin studying the language.

Also, when you do venture into new territory, be sure to create a back-up plan that will catch you if you falter. For example, ask someone you trust to be "on call" to provide you with emotional or practical support in case you need it.

Chapter 9

Instant Gratification

Although it is appropriate for some twentysomethings to quit their day job and leave the country, or pursue adventure full time as a thrilling career, adventure does not necessarily demand such dramatic action. Nor does it require dangerous or reckless behavior. Whether or not you have already made—or are preparing to make—binding commitments involving family, school, career, a mortgage, or heavy debts, you can still invite adventure into your life on a regular basis.

The desire to grow beyond your previous limits can be satisfied in many ways: carving out a bit of time to take that dance class you've been thinking about, asking a new friend out for coffee, picking up a dusty musical instrument, creating a home movie, getting a pet, enrolling in a workshop, designing a new exercise program, volunteering for an organization whose mission speaks to you, or taking a day trip with friends to explore an area near your home. Or adventure could show up in your life as a hobby that enlivens you steadily over time, boosts your spirits, and builds confidence.

A Healthy Drug

The twenties are rife with stress—from the external pressures of making decisions and managing work, finances, school, and relationships, to the internal pressures that gnaw at our self-worth and sow doubts about how we measure up to our peers. This is why it is critical to have something that feeds, supports, and strengthens us on a regular basis.

Mark, twenty-three, relies on martial arts to help him navigate the pressures of his twenties. Raised in a caring home with both parents and two older siblings, Mark began practicing a form of martial arts called Kuk Sool Won when he was in third grade. Although he enjoyed the practice, he dropped it in tenth grade in favor of wrestling. Mark rarely thought about martial arts again until college when, at nineteen, he made a friend who practiced Brazilian Jiu-Jitsu, a martial art and combat sport that focuses on ground fighting.

One day Mark's friend demonstrated a stranglehold on him. Even though Mark had had prior martial arts and wrestling experience, he was powerless to defend himself. Unsettled by this turn of events, he immediately sought to learn more. With his friend's encouragement, he attended some Jiu-Jitsu classes and immediately fell in love with the sport. "Jiu-Jitsu is a highly technical game, like a physical chess match," he says. "It's about understanding your body and being firmly grounded. It was a new, exciting frontier for me." From the start, Mark found that Jiu-Jitsu's benefits went far beyond the studio. Not only did it help him stay in top physical condition, it also helped him maintain mental calm and clarity under stress.

Thanks to a broad interest in the world and a passion for James Bond movies, Mark chose International Relations as his college major, but he did not find it particularly challenging.

111

This changed when he entered graduate school to study international policy. After observing the trends in international politics, he decided to learn Mandarin Chinese in addition to his degree coursework. "I knew learning Chinese would be a smart move for a career in international relations because China could pass America within thirty years," he says.

Learning a foreign language in his early twenties, especially one as difficult as Chinese, has become one of the most difficult challenges Mark has ever faced. To keep his mood up in the face of what sometimes feels like impossible odds, he relies on Jiu-Jitsu:

> Jiu-Jitsu brings out the best in me, the ability to never quit. You learn to hold out when you're being choked and wait for an opportunity to improve your position so you can get out. It's teaching me to exercise all of my options before quitting. This helps me learn Chinese because it's extremely difficult. But if you really want something, even if it's difficult, you need to give yourself the opportunity to keep learning.

While Mark's major challenge at this stage of life is plowing through a heavy graduate course load while also learning Chinese, he acknowledges that twentysomethings struggle with a variety of pressures, from figuring out who they are to finding a good job to navigating intimate relationships. He observes that in the face of such stressors it can be tempting to turn to drugs and alcohol for instant relief. Mark, however, relieves his stress through Jiu-Jitsu:

> Jiu-Jitsu is my drug. It gives me instant gratification and a really good sense of confidence and calm. When I'm training, I have no cares or worries. I completely let go of everything I'm struggling with. After-

wards I feel like I can deal with anything. If I ever get depressed, I focus on Jiu-Jitsu. It keeps me glued together.

Today Mark has been practicing Jiu-Jitsu for four years and wears a purple belt. He trains four nights a week and aims to get his black belt within the next several years. He also competes occasionally because "Every time you compete you learn something, especially where your weaknesses are. Competing is a way I push myself."

Jiu-Jitsu fuels Mark with a constant sense of adventure. He feels that adventure is especially important while we are in our twenties because we are still young and discovering something new about ourselves every day:

Adventure is anything unexpected where you learn about yourself. It could happen at home or during a night out with your friends. It's important to pursue it, though. Don't sit around and wait for adventure to come to you. Put yourself in a position to have it: try new things, take a vacation, move to a new town.

Mark believes the main obstacle that keeps twentysomethings from doing what they want is money. But he encourages us to be creative and not let money stand in the way of following our dreams. "Research is the number one thing," he says. "Don't be lazy. Learn about the opportunities that are out there. Keep looking and use the resources around you." For example, after graduate school Mark is considering applying for the Peace Corps, which allows volunteers to defer most of their student loans while they serve in another country.

Mark recognizes that numerous internal fears also hold us back. He confides one of his own: "Sometimes I'm afraid that by learning Chinese, I'm doing something I'm not especially good at, when I could focus on something else and be better at it." Yet a passion to learn Chinese in order to advance his future career continues to propel him. To move forward in the face of fear, he tells "those thoughts to shut up." Mark shares the approach he finds helpful:

> Relax a little bit. Then get some perspective by looking ahead a year or two and pretend you're looking back on your present self. What advice would your future self have for your present self? Also remember that it's okay to stop moving and look around at your life for a while, or to change course. Sometimes you need to give something up when you find something else that feels better. Find what you really like doing, something that keeps you happy and challenged and stimulates you. And if you feel frustrated, try to hold out and stay with what you enjoy.

To Mark, living your calling means "finding something you're truly good at and using it to contribute to something bigger than yourself." Although he can identify numerous interests, he is not yet sure what his own calling is. But he trusts that this will be revealed in time as long as he stays true to himself and pursues the interests that are meaningful to him.

At this point, Jiu-Jitsu is just Mark's favorite hobby, not a career goal. But he doesn't rule out the possibility of morphing the two together someday. In fact, he dreams of bringing Jiu-Jitsu seminars to China in the future. Although he cannot yet visualize the mechanics of how this could happen—especially since he has a long way to go before he is an expert either in Jiu-Jitsu or Chinese—he is open to the possibility that circumstances will somehow line up to nurture his dream to fruition.

Finally, Jiu-Jitsu has taught Mark to remain centered in the here and now. He's learned that projecting too far into the future can be a hindrance, not a help, to a happy life:

> I don't try to plan everything out or look too far into the future because you can get disconnected from the world when you do that. It's better to just do what you want and not overanalyze it. I'm comfortable keeping my calling broad so I can figure it out as I go along. I hope to influence the world in my own way.

As Mark knows, an adventurous hobby is an excellent way to find relief from stress and develop self-confidence while staying steadily committed to your highest priorities. We all have certain activities we have to do to maintain our sanity and peace of mind. It's important to nurture these activities during your twenties because they change your life for the better, from the inside out. They burn off excess energy, ground you in the present moment, and support your development when you might otherwise be tempted to search for relief in food, alcohol, or drugs. Inserting adventure into your regular routine also adds an element of spontaneity that helps you uncover your true self. By planting these seeds, you might find that they grow from a favorite hobby into much, much more.

QUESTIONS TO CONSIDER

- How do you typically deal with stress? Where do you seek instant gratification?

- Do you have a hobby that regularly relieves your stress and builds your self-esteem?

  ¤ If not, what activities naturally appeal to you?

  ¤ What kind of creative solutions could you come up with to overcome the obstacles that keep you from pursuing these activities?

- Imagine you are looking back at your present-day self from five years in the future. What advice or encouragement could you give your present self?

Chapter 10

Internal Leaps

Adventure is clothed in many external packages, but its gravitational pull comes from deep within. Its source is life's need to create a rite of passage that moves us from one phase of development to the next. At heart, the yearning to be or do something more indicates a fundamental need for a closer connection to ourselves.

I know this to be true from personal experience. Since graduating from high school, my feet have yielded to wanderlust time and again. I have lived in many different places, traveled throughout much of the United States and Europe, held numerous jobs, met countless people from countless backgrounds, and entered into many deeply rewarding relationships. And I don't plan on slowing down any time soon. While these experiences have marked my twenties with vivid color and a wide variety of stories to tell, the biggest rewards have been the internal leaps that have occurred by pushing myself past my comfort zone time and again.

In large part, my urge to bounce around arises from a thirst to draw near to me the people, places, and things that once seemed different and separate, as well as to avoid boredom! Yet on a core level I am driven by something else entirely. In my early twenties I was like a child perpetually afraid to spend the night away from home. Whenever I ventured into new terrain, I was met with insecurity, anxiety, and bouts of depression. Without something familiar to cling to on the outside, I crumbled on the inside. But one day a powerful thought cut like a knife through my fear, awakening a new, clear, internal objective: *I want to be so comfortable in my own skin that I feel at home no matter where I am.*

This ideal instantly gripped me. I accepted the dare to obey my instincts no matter where they led while monitoring my emotional responses for signs of progress. Armed with a newfound focus on inner peace, I began to trust my instincts more frequently and to pick myself up more quickly when I fell. Beneath the adventures that dot my twenties, the most notable one I have taken resides on an intangible level: the personal growth generated by learning to value the call of my heart over the rattle of my fear.

I have learned that adventure challenges us to outgrow the tendency to obsess about everything that could go wrong and directs our attention instead to the love and support that is waiting just around the corner. Whether your actions are small or large, whenever you heed the nudges of your inner voice you offer the little bit of trust that is needed for a shift in consciousness. Then you discover that getting out of your own way and connecting to the natural rhythm of your life leads you to your calling, without struggle or force.

Miraculous Self-Growth

Underneath the glitz and the glamour, the adrenaline and the excitement, the real purpose of adventure—personal growth—gradually reveals itself. You begin to realize you have acquired a new perspective, a calmer response to a situation that previously triggered a strong emotional reaction, a heightened equanimity in the face of the unknown. Sometimes this growth does not reveal itself until you have landed back in your safety net.

When you take a risk and follow your curiosity, you tap into depths of creativity and strength that you may not have known you had. You connect to the flow of life, that ever-present source of energy that provides for you whenever you release your fears long enough to surrender to it. You learn how to give and how to receive (which is just as important). Unexpected sources of support show up in your path just when you need them most.

Emily, a twenty-eight-year-old writer and reporter living in New York City, has learned repeatedly that if she is proactive enough to leap, life will catch her. Growing up in California's Silicon Valley, Emily was a creative child with a natural bent toward writing. During college, she focused on philosophy, art, and humanities. She also interned at a local radio station on the side. After graduating from the University of California, Los Angeles, Emily sensed that she would one day work in media, although she did not know where. At the time she was intrigued by filmmaking, so she stayed put and sought work in Hollywood.

She soon came to appreciate the power of networking. "I met tons of people in the movie industry and the jobs just magically appeared, even though they didn't pay well." In two years she held about eighteen jobs, including gigs as a movie and commercial production assistant and as a talent agent. Over time, however, Emily's enthusiasm for the movie industry and Los Angeles waned. She found herself surrounded by unhappy people and realized that the longer she remained in the middle of negative energy, the lower her own emotions plunged.

Emily packed up and headed for San Francisco, intending to write a memoir about her days working in Hollywood. She wrote the book while supporting herself as a server and bartender. But after completing it, she concluded it was nothing more than a sophomoric attempt at writing, and she tossed it in the trash.

As she recovered from the emotional stress of her early twenties, Emily's interest in radio began to reawaken. She started submitting commentary to local radio stations and accepted a volunteer internship. This led to freelance work for National Public Radio, where some wonderful mentors urged her to become a journalist. Heeding their encouragement, she applied to various radio stations around the country. Because she was broke and in debt, she jumped at the first job offer that came her way: at a public radio network in Alaska.

Emily considers herself an urbanite, so Alaska was not exactly her first choice, but she decided to make the best of it. The good thing about her new job was that her coworkers were tremendously supportive and gave her plenty of time on air as an anchorwoman. The bad thing was that she chafed in Alaska's rustic environment and long, dark winters. After three months of working at the radio network, she again relied on the power of networking to invoke her next opportunity.

During this time, Emily had been a reader of a *Wall Street Journal Online* column about twentysomethings. When the columnist resigned, she wrote a column saying good-bye to her readers. Emily called the managing editor of the website, whom her friend knew, to express her interest in filling the position. Since the managing editor was not in charge of hiring, he gave Emily the name of the woman who was. Emily contacted the woman several times, but never received a reply. Instead of giving up, she got creative. She pitched ten columns and sent them to the woman. The result? She got the job. This was neither the first nor the last time that Emily witnessed how outside forces line up to support us when we really want something, if we are willing to think creatively and take action on our hunches.

Emily spent the next couple of years writing a column about her own generation—first as a freelancer from Alaska, then from New York City, where she also secured a full time job with the *Wall Street Journal* as an online editor. Although Emily's column was a success, her attempts to continue moving up in the news organization were not. After knocking into one dead end after another, she accepted that she would not be able to climb the corporate hierarchy. In reality, she was not particularly fond of corporate values, anyway. When she left, she felt at peace knowing that she had made the right decision.

In the months leading up to her departure from the *Wall Street Journal*, Emily developed a new interest: Africa. She recognized that this region of the world was sorely underreported, and she yearned to go there as a foreign correspondent and write the people's stories. In particular, she was intrigued by Somalia, a war-torn country on the brink of famine. Emily managed to secure an investigative reporting contract with an online magazine so she could travel there firsthand.

Emily prepared for her trip by researching Africa extensively. She even met with scholars at universities, and officials from the U.S. State and Defense Departments. She decided to travel first to Kenya, then to the Somali capital of Mogadishu. Even though she lacked health insurance and had little in savings, her intuition that she *had* to go overrode all factors that seemed to hold her back.

Upon arriving in Kenya, Emily moved into a house with other foreign correspondents from all over the world. But her plans to travel to Mogadishu quickly derailed when she learned that she would have to pay five hundred dollars a day for security to prevent assassination and kidnapping attempts in the lawless, corrupt, and extremely dangerous city. Compounding her stress, her money grew precariously low and she suffered from culture shock:

I was miserable for two months. I went through a period of deprivation where I lost fifteen pounds, and I'd get upset and cry. I wanted to talk to my friends, use the Internet, and go home. You feel like you're at the end of the world, but there's a turning point. You learn to rely on yourself.

This period of loss and confusion eventually passed. Relying on her ingenuity once again, Emily changed course and decided that instead of visiting Mogadishu, she would travel to Somaliland, a relatively peaceful breakaway state in the north of Somalia. There she would conduct as many interviews as possible and hope that her articles would still be worthy of publication.

Upon arriving in Somaliland, Emily found a driver and a local guide who agreed to assist her with her travel and interpretation needs. Then she started interviewing people "like crazy." From nomads to psychiatrists to former warlords, she met with dozens of Somalis to explore the core issues fueling Somalia's seemingly endless conflict. With a hint of awe in her voice, she recalls:

I was my own boss in a way I'd never thought possible before. I had to be extremely creative to get the articles done without going to Mogadishu, so I networked constantly. I borrowed bulletproof vests from the *New York Times* because I couldn't afford them for myself. It took a lot of creative thinking to accomplish everything I'd set out to do, but in the end my articles were accepted.

Unfortunately, just one week after arriving in Somaliland, Emily's money completely ran out. Although this easily could have been a breaking point, she fought the urge to panic. And she was soon rescued by the kindness of the Somalis:

> I had the most amazing experience in Somaliland. The people there never get visitors so they treated me like an honored guest. They thought God had sent me to them. They completely took care of me, drove me around for free, and paid for everything I needed. It was unbelievable to me that it's okay to not be able to take care of yourself.

In spite of the Somalis' generosity, Emily still faced a nine hundred dollar debt—for her hotel bill, her driver, and other expenses she had accumulated—that had to be paid if she was going to leave the country on schedule. Drawing once again on her creative problem-solving abilities, she posted an urgent request on her blog for twenty dollars from each of her friends. She framed her plea not only as a personal favor, but also as a donation to the cause of obtaining original news from Africa.

To Emily's enormous relief, her support network rapidly gathered together the funds she needed. Yet she still faced the challenge of actually receiving the funds. Although by this time she had a growing belief that everything would fall into place, she waited anxiously for the money to arrive. "I'd go to the bank every afternoon and sometimes cry when the money wasn't there." Luckily it did arrive—right before she was supposed to leave.

After three months in Kenya and one month in Somaliland, Emily caught her flight out of Africa as a deeply transformed human being. While she had received support in the past from various people, this adventure raised her trust and belief in the flow of life to an entirely new level and dramatically shifted her perspective:

Going to Africa was a miraculous experience of self-growth. It changed my whole life. If I went to Africa for a few months every year, I wouldn't be competitive, greedy, or depressed. If you're depressed, go to Africa! The people are incredibly optimistic even though they're so poor. The whole experience taught me to believe in miracles.

Emily thinks a calling is spiritual in nature. Her own calling threads throughout her life and gives her reason to get up every morning:

A calling is the gifts you have by the time you become an adult—genetic or developed through family influence and education. You're meant to develop your gifts and use them to enjoy your life and give back to society. My calling is to tell people's stories. When I wake up in the morning, what excites me is the prospect of creating something new. I love being creative; it keeps me interested in my life.

Emily believes the core struggle that twentysomethings have in discovering their life purpose stems from indecision in the face of so many options. Yet she says, "Indecision is actually insecurity and lack of self-confidence." Emily suspects that most of us know more about what we want than we admit to ourselves. The problem is that we are chained by our fears, especially the fear of what other people will think of us if we follow our heart.

"The best thing that can happen," she says, "is to have people react to you in the worst way possible. Then you realize it's not so bad." At the same time, she is quick to point out that the struggle of indecision is also a privilege when looked at in a different light. Young people in impoverished regions of the world do not have a wide array of options at their disposal; their energy is focused on helping themselves and their families survive.

I remarked to Emily that she seemed to possess an unusual ability to follow her instincts without "getting in her own way." She acknowledged that this was true at a certain level, but she added that she has always struggled with money. "There've been times that I was broke and in debt, and I'd shake every morning about money. But I figure it's worth it to be irresponsible for a while to go after what I want."

To discover what it is that we want, Emily suggests that we pay close attention to our thoughts and feelings:

> You have to feel good in the thing you choose. The more I learned about Africa, the more obsessed and fascinated I became. It seemed absolutely necessary to go. Once you've found the next step you want to take—the step that feels good and rewarding—you need to pay attention to the destructive voices in your head that say things like, "What if I go broke? What about my 401k? What if my dad doesn't approve?" Those destructive voices are the devil on my shoulder. They tell you not to do the thing you really should do. I try to ignore them and focus on going forward.

Since returning to New York, Emily has published numerous articles on the war in Somalia. She has also written a memoir of her trip, which her agent is currently shopping around to publishers, and she recently applied for a peace-keeping mission to Ethiopia with the United Nations. "The universe really will support you," she says. "But now it's my turn to be generous and give back to the universe."

Although the essence of Emily's calling is telling other people's stories, her inner voice continues to direct her to new paths. Through this process, she has learned that creative thinking and innovative action play a critical role in finding and following our calling and helping us overcome what at first appear to be overwhelming obstacles.

Cultivating an adventurous spirit does not mean you have to enter a war-torn country with dwindling funds and no health insurance. But it does mean that you open yourself to the opportunity to grow. Whenever you feel unhappy or bored with your life, taking some kind of action—small or large—can help you break out of your familiar routine and rediscover yourself. The struggles and triumphs inherent in exploring this new terrain help you discover new skills and grow in self-confidence. They also show you that life will support you in unexpected, sometimes even magical, ways. In order to experience this transformation, acknowledge that every experience is here to teach you something, allow yourself to think outside the box, and take the first step.

QUESTIONS TO CONSIDER

- Reflect on the last time you accepted your heart's call toward adventure and stepped outside of your comfort zone.

    ¤ What challenges did you face? How did you overcome them?

    ¤ How did you grow internally? How did you change for the better?

    ¤ Were there any unexpected benefits? For example, did you inspire someone else to try something new, too?

- Think of the most adventurous people you know.

  - How do they make decisions? Deal with fear?

  - How can you apply their approach to your own life?

Part 4

Relationships

How You're Called to Connect

Chapter 11

Transitions with Your Parents

In this section I will focus on how to create relationships that support you in following your calling. By this I mean the kind of relationships that nurture your true self and support your deepest desires. Such relationships make you feel safe enough to express yourself freely, inspire you to grow, and allow you to change over time.

The twenties bring newfound autonomy and freedom. After leaving high school, some of us continue to live at home; others pursue higher education or go travel; others settle quickly into the working world. As we shed the skin of childhood and adolescence, we enter a state of suspension: we are no longer who we used to be, but we do not yet fully inhabit the person we are becoming, either. Our relationships bring this uncomfortable reality to light, and often with a fair amount of drama.

During this period of life, it is normal to consider more and more deeply who you are, what you have to give, and who you want surrounding and influencing you. You start to become aware that some people enliven you while others drain you; you discover hobbies and interests that make you happy and seek friends with whom you can share them; and you undergo internal transformations that shed light on your life purpose. Such personal changes inevitably bring changes in your key relationships including those with your parents, longtime friends, and intimate partners.

Naturally this transitional time presents an unsettling, even frightening, dilemma: do you embrace the changes or try to suppress them? If you are too afraid of hurting or losing someone, of shaking up comfortable—yet outdated—patterns, you may resist your own instincts. This can lead to periods of confusion, stagnation, even depression.

Over time, these forces can bring some of your relationships to the boiling point. How do you balance who you used to be with the person you are becoming? How do you create the relationships you want, even if you've been hurt in the past? How do you find community when change is constant? This tension serves an important purpose because it causes you to withdraw your attention from the outside world and search inside for the answers.

During this process, try to stay connected to your inner voice and embrace change even in spite of your fears. It's true that your relationships during this stage of life will change; some might even disappear altogether. When they do, find ways to be gentle with yourself and allow your emotions to surface. Then focus on moving forward, all the while anticipating the happiness you will experience when wonderful new relationships enter your life or when your existing relationships develop into something even richer than they were before.

It's Your Life

As we transition from dependent children to independent adults, the relationships with our parents necessarily change. For practical purposes, I'll use the word *parents* to indicate the living caretaker(s) with whom we maintain contact. Today's twentysomethings experience so many different models of the parent-child relationship that it's impossible to make sweeping generalizations. Some of us are close to one or both parents and view them as friends or role models, while others have strained or estranged relationships. Some of us are still financially dependent on our parents, while others are completely independent of them. Some of us live far away, while others live just down the hall. Some of us were raised by our grandparents or foster parents. Some of our parents are struggling with serious illness. Others of us have lost one or both parents to death.

The parental relationship is particularly profound because it strongly affects our development and orientation in the world. Children naturally rely on their parents for their very survival. Whether or not you got along well with your parents, you probably viewed them as elevated figures and absorbed their outlook on life, their actions, even their emotions. Until you uncover your true self, you might continually make choices that either reflect or rebel against your parents' values and beliefs, even if they are not really your own. You might even abandon your own path in an attempt to please your parents, and then wonder why you aren't happy.

Sometimes our parents have hopes or expectations for our lives that do not align with our own vision. For example, your parents might want you to practice their religion, be heterosexual, live close to home, marry within your race, have children by a certain age, or follow a particular career track. They might even want you to be constantly available to meet their needs beyond your ability or desire to do so.

In the face of pressures that do not feel right, it's important to be honest with yourself and your parents about your own priorities and the direction in which you want to take your life. Even if you love and appreciate your parents deeply, you may enter into a period of confusion, dancing back and forth between old patterns of interaction and new ones as you redefine the relationship with them. During this time, it's normal to take two steps forward and one step back, to suddenly feel like a child again just when you are trying to establish yourself as an adult.

Marie, twenty-seven, has had to untangle herself from her parents' expectations in order to follow her calling. She grew up in a close, loving home with her parents' marriage intact. Her father thrived in his position as an executive in the banking industry, where he accumulated substantial wealth. Her mother worked as a teacher, although she was never very happy in the profession.

During college, Marie pursued her love of writing and obtained a degree in English. After graduation, however, she became interested in earning a lot of money, so she went into the banking industry like her father. Both of her parents were pleased with this career choice and encouraged her to work hard in order to climb the corporate ladder. Yet unlike her father, Marie grew increasingly unhappy with her career. By her mid-twenties she was miserable and dreaded going to work each morning.

As she began to question why she was so unhappy, Marie realized that she was living outside of her true nature. She believes that a calling is "what you were made to do" and that her own calling lies in cultivating meaningful relationships with others. It dawned on her that "Even though I talk to people every day as a banker, I don't have many satisfying conversations."

This realization spurred her to brainstorm a career path that might be more fulfilling. She searched her memory for the times when she had felt most truly alive, which cleared a space for her inner voice to emerge. Images began to percolate in her mind about service trips she had taken in her youth, high school teachers who had inspired her, and her love of writing. She soon realized that she wanted to go back to school to become a high school English teacher:

> I don't have grandiose notions about changing the world or feeling passionate all the time. But teaching is about dedication to kids and helping them through the difficult things they're going through. I mean, life can be rough for them. It's important to me to build relationships like that.

Unfortunately, Marie's parents did not share her enthusiasm for her new career plans. "My dad is all about practicality," she says. "He kept going on about how I'd be financially set for the rest of my life if I stayed in banking, and that I shouldn't leave because I'm so good at it." She sighs, "I know he meant well—he just wants me to be taken care of—but it was frustrating." Marie's mother struggled to support her decision as well, especially since she had not found lasting satisfaction in her own career as a teacher.

Marie mulled over her parents' advice, but in the end she resolved to follow her inner guidance. "I finally told them that the point isn't that I'm good at banking or that I'll make a lot of money. The point is I don't like banking and I'm not going to change my mind." Once they saw how determined she was to pursue teaching, her parents began to respect her decision.

Today Marie is finishing both her graduate program in education and her days as a banker. As she begins to apply for teaching jobs, she has no regrets. She has learned an important lesson: giving too much weight to the opinions of others, even those as close to us as our parents, can distract us from our own path:

It's important to bounce ideas off of other people, but ultimately it's your life. Nobody knows you better than you do. Everyone thinks they know what's best for you, but you have to go with your feelings and then deal with the consequences. I'm not concerned about what other people think of me anymore because my priorities are clear.

Resolving Conflict

As you work through growing pains with your own family, you might come to appreciate your parents more fully than you used to and even become close friends with them. You might also develop a new compassion for their humanity, what they have gone through in life, and the sacrifices they have made for you.

Or you might realize that the turbulence you experience with your parents relates not only to present-day disagreements, but to longstanding, unresolved issues. Perhaps you have been avoiding a particular subject because you are afraid that—if you address it—you will struggle to express yourself, or you will hurt your parents' feelings, or you might even jeopardize the entire relationship. But if you fail to acknowledge your parents' influence on you, you could struggle to find happiness in life and not know why.

This occurs because the relationships with your parents have shaped you from the very beginning of your life and affect you at the core of your being. If you are storing years of pent-up tension, your perceptions and emotions may have become so clouded that you battle depression or unconsciously stir up problems in other areas of your life, from work to intimate relationships. In other words, you could find yourself constantly bogged down by symptoms whose source you never address.

To free yourself from these blockages, start by acknowledging that as an adult, you are now responsible for your own health and well-being. Yes, you were influenced by the environment in which you grew up and may have accumulated burdens that weigh you down. Now it's time to find ways to release the negatives and to heal yourself by making different, more empowering choices in the present moment where your power lies.

If it feels appropriate, you may want to initiate a candid conversation with your parents to air the difficult issues that are still unresolved. If it doesn't feel right, you may just need to move on and find other methods of healing. For your own well-being, you may also need to set boundaries with your parents that you have been previously reluctant to enforce. And if you need additional support in dealing with family relationships, consider seeking professional help.

Because discussions surrounding hot-button topics can be painful and heated, keep the following tips in mind while moving forward with your parents. These tips can apply to other relationships, too.

Choose a neutral time and place

If possible, bring up important topics with your parents in person. Try to address your concerns while you are together in a relaxed environment, rather than waiting until tensions erupt and you are in the midst of an argument. Calm settings can help to reduce defensiveness and make it easier for everyone to think and respond more clearly to the issues at hand.

If it's not possible to talk with your parents in person, or if it doesn't feel right to do so, consider writing them a letter or initiating a discussion over the phone.

Pave the way for success

Since none of us have control over our parents' responses, decide in advance that you will consider the conversation a success no matter what the outcome is. Create a safe mental space that will give you courage and comfort later, such as "Regardless of how Dad reacts when I bring up this topic with him, I'm going to give myself credit for trying. The conversation will be a success because I made the effort to get things out in the open and improve our relationship."

In this way you do not abdicate your happiness to forces outside of your control, and you create a supportive internal space to return to after the conversation is over.

Present your position

Before approaching your parents, search inwardly to gain clarity about what you really need to say. You may first want to write a letter that you don't send, or talk through your feelings with a therapist or close friend. When you do talk with your parents, try to present your point of view without being defensive or blaming them. Share what is in your heart simply and straightforwardly. State the way you feel and what you need to do to be happy or take care of yourself.

Let your parents know if you want something from them, such as support or understanding. At the same time, be clear inside yourself that they are not responsible for your peace of mind. You are.

Accept your parents

Just as you have a right to your own thoughts and feelings, so do your parents. Try not to approach these conversations with the mindset of trying to "make" them see things the way you do. Nobody will understand you all the time, including your parents, and it's helpful to accept this fact in advance.

Do your best to listen to your parents' position with an open mind, and without interrupting them. Take into consideration the factors that have shaped their viewpoint and see if you can find common ground.

Express appreciation

If you can, open and close the discussion on a note of appreciation. Let your parents know that you value them and tell them how they have made a positive difference in your life. Appreciation can set a respectful, positive tone that makes it easier to work through difficult matters.

Letting go

When dealing with stressful situations with loved ones, keep in mind that people and situations often change over time. Naturally it can be tempting to seek a "quick fix" to a painful relationship dynamic. But sometimes the best option is to speak your truth with compassion, and then step back and just allow the relationship to *be*. You might be surprised at what happens when you relax and let go a little.

When communication is not an option

While open communication with our parents can be a big help, it's not always the best option—or even possible. Some twentysomethings are in situations with their parents that are especially distressing, and they decide to approach their personal healing in other ways. If you decide not to address difficult subjects directly with your parents, you can still evaluate the situation honestly, commit to taking good care of yourself, and act in ways that honor your own well-being. At the same time, be sure to reach out for support as you need it from a therapist, support group, mentor, or friend. It is also a good idea to find a creative outlet that allows you to safely express your emotions as you move forward with your life.

In the long run, your emotional freedom serves your parents' growth as well as your own because it gives them the opportunity to liberate themselves from the past and live more fully in the present. Ideally, an open and honest assessment will help each person in the relationship make peace. If it is impossible to achieve this with your parents, at least you can achieve it within yourself. Healing your parental relationships releases enormous amounts of energy that have been tightly bound in old, conflicted emotions. This brings you new levels of clarity, creativity, and confidence that you can then harness to create a life you love.

QUESTIONS TO CONSIDER

- Reflect on your relationships with your parents.

  ◻ How would you describe the dynamics between you?

  ◻ What are two or three messages that you have internalized from your parents about yourself or the world?

  ◻ Have you suppressed any desires because you didn't want to let your parents down?

  ◻ How often do you express your love and appreciation to them?

- Is there any underlying tension with one or both parents that you have avoided dealing with directly?

◻ How has this tension affected your personality and other areas of your life, such as your work and intimate relationships?

◻ Would you consider addressing the issue openly with your parents? If so, consider the tips mentioned earlier in the chapter.

◻ If you are not comfortable opening up a discussion either in person or over the phone, consider writing your parents a letter. This can be a great way to express yourself because you have plenty of time to reflect on what you really need to say, and you can revise your words until they accurately reflect what's in your heart.

◻ If you conclude that open communication is not the best option, what do you need to make peace within yourself? More support from others? Better self-care? Would it help to write a letter to your parents that you don't send, just to express your feelings?

Chapter 12

Navigating Friendships

Friendship is important at every stage of life. It is particularly important in our twenties because we are undergoing so many internal and external changes. We need support and encouragement when we succeed, and empathy and compassion when we falter. We yearn for a network of people with whom we can share good times, rely on during tough times, and call on for emotional and practical support. Close friends can provide the solace we seek; they can even be so important that they feel like our chosen family. Yet we are also in the midst of a powerful transition that inevitably leads to shifting dynamics in all relationships, not the least of which is our friendships.

Despite your best attempts to keep in touch with friends from different periods of your life, you might struggle to find the right balance. Leaving school (high school, college, or other) can propel you into an unfamiliar social world, even if you remain in your hometown. No longer protected by the familiar cocoon that school provided, you might start to feel lonely and insecure, and struggle to find new friends and build community.

During this time, you might also discover that some old friendships are no longer as satisfying as they used to be. This can happen when you and your friends form diverging world-views, pursue new interests and activities, or enter different phases of life. For example, some of us are getting married while others remain single; some of us are planting roots in one community while others are moving to totally new locations. Some of us are having children; others are climbing the career ladder at full speed; still others refuse to settle down at all. Sometimes chance plays a role in the equation, too. A serious medical diagnosis, death in the family, or dramatic and unforeseen event can catapult us in entirely new directions.

In the midst of change, it can be tempting to cling to the way things used to be and attempt to recreate a previous dynamic that no longer exists. You might start to feel threatened if your friends become more empowered than you are or if they are moving away from you in some way. Similarly, they could fear losing you if you are headed in a new direction. You might need to initiate an honest conversation to discuss the changes and see if you can move into the future together. Or you might sense that the changes are just too great and that it's time to let the friendship go.

If you find yourself in the uncomfortable position of breaking up with a friend, allow yourself to feel the residual sadness and/or anger and process the loss as you would any other breakup. While letting go, ask yourself what purpose the relationship served and try to acknowledge the positive qualities that your friend brought into your life. Even if you do go separate ways, remember that words and demeanor are powerful. We can tear each other down or lift each other up with the smallest comments and actions. Regardless of the circumstances, you can still communicate your truth with kindness, keep your heart open, and encourage your friend's success (even if only silently).

Over time, as you come to terms with who you are, you

will probably deepen the connection with some longtime friends and let others go. You will also meet new friends with whom you can walk into the next phase of life. The potential for connection and friendship is ever-present; we just need to stay open to it, even in the most unlikely places. Whenever you feel alone or unsteady, remember that companionship could be just around the corner.

Removing Your Mask

Alicia, twenty-seven, grew up in a small suburban apartment with her mother and grandmother. As the only black student in her all-white class at a Catholic school, she secretly felt that she did not fit in anywhere. During high school, a popular girl took Alicia under her wing. By observing the way her friend interacted with others, Alicia learned how she could blend in at school. To ensure her social success, she studiously avoided conflict with her peers. She also developed a sunny, bubbly personality and made many new friends.

Yet underneath the surface, Alicia felt deep pain related to family troubles and her struggle for identity. She did not share this pain even with her closest friends because she feared they would not understand her problems or, even worse, that they would make insensitive comments. "Everyone knew I smiled and laughed a lot," she says, "but even my best friends didn't know about my sad side."

Soon after Alicia graduated from college, her beloved grandmother grew gravely ill. Alicia could not bear to be away from her grandmother when she was sick, so she made a decision that launched her into a vastly different life stage than that of her peers: she moved back home to become her grandmother's full time caretaker. While her friends were starting careers, dating, and traveling, Alicia spent her days lifting her grandmother up and down the stairs and helping her with basic functions such as getting dressed, taking medicine, and paying bills. "Sometimes I felt like my friends didn't understand what I was going through," Alicia says, "but looking back I see I didn't give them a chance to understand."

When Alicia was in her mid-twenties, her grandmother died. Although she felt shattered, she was also at a turning point. It gradually dawned on her that she had a gift for understanding and supporting others. She came to realize that her calling was not only about honoring others' truths, but also about sharing her own. "Your calling includes your relationships because you learn about different parts of yourself with different people," she says. "My calling has to do with understanding and honest communication, getting to the truth in every situation."

As Alicia emerged from grief, she began to build a new life by getting a full time job and reenergizing her social life. She identified the interests that brought her the most fulfillment: personal growth, healing, writing, and socializing with others through shared activities. Because she was willing to stretch beyond her comfort zone and attend events by herself, she joined support groups, writing groups, and social clubs. She also sought out lectures and meetings on interesting topics, such as those involving inspirational speakers, women in business, and international affairs. And she began spending time with new friends from work.

During this stage of her life, Alicia grew and expanded rapidly. She met people with whom she felt safe to share herself freely, people who drew her out in the way that she naturally drew others out. As a result, she began to take risks with her new friends and to share herself more openly and authentically than she had done in the past. Expressing her true self helped her feel lighter and happier. "We blossom in safe relationships," she says. "When I'm not wearing a mask my stomach feels clear, not anxious, like I'm 'in the zone.' And my conversations are awesome."

As Alicia developed more self-confidence, she became aware that she needed to be more honest with her old friends, too. Not long ago, Nicole, whom she has known since childhood, got upset because Alicia failed to return her calls promptly and showed up late for plans they had made. Nicole's frustrations pointed to issues that had been festering underneath the surface of their friendship for a while.

In contrast to her old pattern of automatically acquiescing and apologizing whenever anyone took issue with her, Alicia decided to approach the conflict openly. "I e-mailed Nicole and spoke up for my position. I told her I understood what she was saying, but I also felt hurt and misunderstood about a few things." To Alicia's happiness, Nicole responded supportively. "She really considered my point of view," Alicia says. "She even told me she loves it when I share my feelings and wishes I'd do it more often. It actually brought us closer together." This was a big milestone for Alicia because it helped her realize that she could express her true self even with her friends from childhood.

Today Alicia's life is filled with supportive friends (old and new) who support her dream of becoming a counselor. Even better, they value truthful communication as much as she does. Now she understands that we need to address, rather than avoid, conflict with our friends if we feel misunderstood or unsupported. She also recognizes that people come into our lives for a purpose and that sometimes friendships end. "I used to feel so sad if I knew someone and then we didn't talk anymore," she says, "but now I know it's okay to move on. Even if you're sad about losing someone, it doesn't necessarily mean something went wrong."

Alicia's advice

If you would like to make supportive new friends, but you don't know how or where to start, here is the approach that worked for Alicia:

> Start by figuring out what you like to do, then attend a meeting or join a group. Bring an open, positive attitude wherever you go and take interest in the people around you. Be willing to share yourself, including your vulnerabilities. And don't classify people in a way that puts up barriers to friendship. For me, since I'm single, I used to get jealous of my friends who are in relationships—but I had to let that go so my jealousy didn't separate us. This also applies if you're a woman and you think you can't be friends with men, or if people are older than you, or from a different country, or in a different stage of life. Categorizing people makes us feel safe, but it also keeps us lonely. Pay attention when you feel a genuine connection with someone. You never know who has value to add to your life or who might become a friend.

Alicia believes that the Internet provides excellent tools for networking and for keeping in touch with people you already know, but she does not believe it should be used as a substitute for human contact:

> It can be tempting for people in their twenties to hide behind online masks when they feel lonely inside. You can be whoever you want online and that can create an illusion of connection. But there's a difference between really connecting with someone and making an online contact. You can have fifty Facebook friends

147

and still feel lonely. I mean, you can't get a hug from your computer.

Finally, Alicia has concluded that if you want to follow your calling, it is important to have friends by your side who wholeheartedly support and encourage you in becoming your best self, rather than friends who ignore, inhibit, or discourage your growth. "Your vision for your life includes your relationships," she says. "Every one of them is a gift, so nurture the good ones because they're definitely worth your time."

As Alicia has learned, creating fulfilling friendships during this decade involves updating old relationships into present time, and also being assertive about meeting new people who share your values. Even if you undergo periods of discomfort with old friends, these transitions can actually help your relationships become more rewarding than they were before. In order to reach a positive outcome, allow yourself and your friends to change. Try to embrace the people you have become today. Ultimately, the process of navigating friendships molds you into a person who is more available for intimacy in every area of life.

QUESTIONS TO CONSIDER

- Which of your friends supports your dreams, makes you feel good about who you are, and encourages your growth without reservation?

- Do any of your friends drag you down through drama, negativity, or guilt?

◻ If you have not already done so, do you need to address the issue directly?

• Are you clinging to a friendship or pattern of interaction because you are afraid of change or loss?

◻ If so, how can you allow this relationship to move into its next, natural phase?

• Do you want to draw more supportive friends into your life?

◻ If you do, consider Alicia's advice.

Chapter 13

Dating and Intimacy

Intimate relationships tend to be the most emotionally intense and revealing ones we have in our twenties. They are especially complex because so many unseen forces converge in them, including our self-esteem (or lack thereof), our past traumas and rejections, our hopes for the future, and our life purpose. When it comes to dating and intimacy, twentysomething relationships take many different forms such as gay, straight, lesbian, and bisexual. We are in monogamous relationships or open relationships. We are happy to be single or unhappily single. We would like to get married one day or have no desire to do so. Others are married, or have already been married and divorced.

To create and maintain intimate relationships that nourish your true self, reflect on the following principle: intimate relationships help you heal internal wounds and fulfill your potential. But this does not mean they are always easy. Relationships help you grow by mirroring your strengths as well as the places in which you are emotionally "stuck." This means that your partner's actions, or the actions of the people you are attracted to, can trigger you in a way that pushes you to see yourself more clearly. For example, if you repeatedly feel frustrated, bored, neglected, or jealous in your intimate relationships, there may be an aspect of your own self-esteem that needs attention. Through these experiences and reflections, you will learn what you need to heal within yourself, even if it is difficult to look at.

When working through a healing process, it is helpful to explore the family dynamics in which you grew up. Unexamined, the roles you played in your family and the patterns of interaction considered normal during your formative years will move with you into adulthood. Human beings tend to recreate similar emotional scenes in different places with different faces because they feel comfortable, normal, like home—even if they also cause a great deal of suffering.

When the same patterns repeat over and over again in your intimate relationships, it is probably a sign that a core pattern you learned in childhood is still active within you. For example, unresolved tension with one of your parents could lead you to experience a chronic problem in your dating life. You might find yourself continually attracted to people who are emotionally needy or unavailable, or getting upset with your partner over a frustration that actually originated when you were very young.

These recurring patterns indicate that there is something important to uncover within yourself in order to create more fulfilling relationships with others. Maybe you need to attend to your emotions, address a relationship conflict more directly, or change a behavioral pattern that is holding love at bay. Recognizing these simple truths provides the opportunity to move beyond your past by choosing to feel and act differently in the present.

Wake-Up Calls

Ideally, intimate relationships give you direct support for your growth and dreams. At other times, they serve as wake-up calls that show you that you have been looking to a partner for affirmation instead of affirming yourself. Although wake-up calls often involve a painful event, they can shake you up so much that you are forced to take a good look at your life, unplug from the patterns that are not making you happy, and reconnect to your true self. When you approach intimate relationships consciously—that is to say, when you take responsibility for your own part in them—you pave the way for more happiness and less drama in the future.

Jill, twenty-nine, has learned how an intimate relationship can serve as a wake-up call. "For most of my twenties, I was in a relationship where I ignored my gut feeling that something was wrong," she says. She now knows how important it is to listen to her inner voice.

Jill was born to teenaged parents. They tried hard to make their relationship work, but over time they grew apart due to their young age and her father's drinking. Eventually they divorced. Jill's mother soon remarried, and the family moved out-of-state. This was very painful for Jill because it separated her from the only home and friends she had ever known. Over the years, Jill's father continued to hold down a job, but he slipped further into alcoholism with each passing year.

Because she had watched her mother's struggles with an alcoholic husband, Jill swore to herself from a young age that she would never put herself in the same situation. She also developed strong tendencies to nurture others:

> I played the role of "nurturer" in my family. Growing up, I would try and comfort my mom and dad whenever they were upset, and they would do the same with me. It's an innate part of my personality to take care of people, and I also learned it from family members who are the same way.

As Jill entered her twenties, her determination to never enter into a relationship with an alcoholic strengthened, as did her habit of putting others' needs ahead of her own. She met her boyfriend, Brad, when she was in her early twenties. One of the major pluses for her was that Brad did not drink alcohol. Even so, she now recognizes that her father's alcoholism was still affecting her just underneath the surface. "It was a huge attraction to me that Brad didn't drink," she says, "but I've realized now that this was a protective mechanism and shouldn't have been such a weighing factor." By overemphasizing one quality she wanted in a partner, she overlooked the fact that other important qualities she was looking for were missing.

"Brad was my project," she says. "We went through a lot together. I supported him whenever he needed help." Yet a gut feeling nagged at her again and again: *Is this really the right man for me?* But she ignored it. Her intuition was too threatening to acknowledge at the time. It suggested that she make bigger changes than she was ready for, such as possibly leaving Brad.

After several years of dating, the couple decided to marry. Jill enthusiastically planned an elegant, catered wedding. It was a beautiful event, filled with love, laughter, family, and friends. But not long after the festivities ended, Jill was overcome by a sudden outburst of tears while she was at home with Brad one day. She convinced herself (and Brad) that she was crying because she missed her family. But that was not the full truth. She admits now that "I wasn't getting the emotional support I needed and felt all alone in the marriage."

One day Jill was going through the telephone bill and saw a series of late-night calls to a number she did not recognize. On impulse, she dialed the number. When a woman's voice answered, she said, "I believe you know my husband, Brad. What type of relationship do you have with him?" The

woman denied anything beyond a possible business association. When Jill saw Brad later that day, she asked him the
same question. Although he initially denied any wrongdoing,
he eventually confessed that he had had an affair.

Jill was devastated. Despite her previous conviction that
"marriage is forever," she decided to file for divorce. It was
an excruciating time, but one that proved to be a powerful
catalyst for her personal awakening. Although she was hurt
and angry, she did not blame Brad for everything. Instead,
she accepted responsibility for her own part in the dissolution
of her marriage.

Jill knew that the moment she saw the suspicious numbers
on the phone bill was not the first time she had recognized
that something was seriously wrong. She also realized that she
had been so focused on nurturing Brad that she had fallen
further and further away from her true self:

> Now that I'm divorced, I can see that I gave a lot emo-
> tionally without it being reciprocated. I've learned
> that I'm a "giver," which is fine, but I need to make
> sure that I'm getting out of a relationship what I'm
> putting in. Also, it's important for me to see people
> for who they really are and accept that, versus seeing
> them for who I think they could be or should be, or
> who I could help them be. Now I know I deserve
> more in a relationship and I will not settle for less in
> the future.

As Jill became aware of the unhealthy ways in which the
role of nurturer had played out in her life, she also became
aware of the flip side: her gift for nurturing others was actually
her calling when directed in a more conscious way. "My calling
is my compassion for people," Jill says, "especially a desire
to work with kids and help them build their self-esteem."

She returned to this first love and began volunteering with a program that assists children and their parents.

During this time, Jill also focused on nurturing herself. She exercised regularly, cultivated supportive friendships, and blossomed in the career she loves. Through the process of discovering who she is and accepting herself at a deeper level than ever before, Jill became clear about what she wanted in her next relationship: a man who was emotionally available, financially stable, and committed to his own—as well as her—personal growth.

With her clear intentions, she attracted a wonderful man with whom she is now in a happy, committed relationship. Together they prioritize open communication and taking good care of themselves and each other. Jill also accepts that her boyfriend drinks socially from time to time. She no longer reacts to her dad's addiction in such a way that she requires a partner who doesn't drink at all.

Jill feels that twentysomethings need to focus on their personal growth first and that problems arise in relationships when we ignore our intuition:

> I think a lot of twentysomethings stay in constant relationships to avoid loneliness. A common struggle seems to be that they're still working on finding themselves, but they're also looking to others to make them happy and fulfilled. What they really need is to take time to understand what makes them happy first. Another struggle is not wanting to fail. I stayed in a relationship longer than I should have because I didn't want to give up and feel that I had failed at something I had worked so hard at. Now I know this is an attitude that can do more harm than good.

Jill advises twentysomethings to believe in themselves and trust their gut instincts when it comes to their intimate relationships. "You never know what's around the corner, so stay confident in yourself," she says. "Instead of having regrets, learn from your past decisions and let them help shape your future. It all makes you a stronger person."

Values and Deal Breakers

As Jill's story illustrates, if you desire an intimate relationship that supports you and inspires you to become your best self, it is important to focus on your own personal growth first and foremost. As you do, consider the factors from your upbringing that have affected your emotional development and the way you approach intimate relationships. It is also a good idea to clarify the qualities you most want in a partner and those you cannot tolerate. This means identifying your values and deal breakers.

In contrast to a hobby, which is an activity you enjoy doing but do not necessarily have to share with a partner, a *value* is something that is so important to you, so fundamental to the way you approach life, that you might never be fully satisfied in a relationship with someone who does not share it. For example, two of Jill's values are emotional availability and open communication. After experiencing their opposite, she now knows that these two qualities must be present for her to feel satisfied in an intimate relationship. Other examples of values could include a similar cultural/religious/spiritual orientation, the desire to have children, intellectual curiosity, honesty, affection, sustainable living, or even political affiliation.

In the process of clarifying your values, you will also come across their opposite: *deal breakers*. These are qualities you simply cannot accept in a long-term, intimate relationship.

Clearly, for Jill a deal breaker was cheating, which was the catalyst that caused her to leave her husband. For others, deal breakers could include substance addiction, verbal or physical abuse, lying, emotional neglect, closed-mindedness, controlling behavior, or lack of physical attraction. In contrast to things that aggravate you but that can be resolved through discussion and compromise (such as when your partner does not clean up at home), deal breakers are the things you cannot overlook. In the long run, they prevent you from being truly happy in a partnership.

Finally, when you begin to understand how your intimate relationships mirror the things you most need to heal in yourself, it becomes clear that they are sacred vehicles through which you evolve. Because they serve such a profound purpose, they are never failures, regardless of how they turn out or how long they last. The true measures of success are the lessons you learn and the depth to which you allow yourself to grow.

QUESTIONS TO CONSIDER

- What role did you play in your family growing up?

  - Do you have a tendency to play this same role in your intimate relationships?

  - If so, how does it positively and negatively affect your relationships?

  - If you feel stuck in this role, how can you begin moving beyond it?

- Reflect on your past relationships.

- ◻ Can you detect a theme or pattern as to why they did not work out?

- ◻ What have you learned to do differently?

- If you are in a relationship right now, how supportive is your partner of your personal growth? How much support do you offer your partner in return?

- What are your most important values and deal breakers in an intimate relationship?

- Take a moment to visualize your ideal relationship.

  - ◻ What are the qualities of your partner?

  - ◻ How do you interact with one another? How do you spend your time together?

  - ◻ How do you look, carry yourself, and most importantly, feel when you are with this person?

  - ◻ Now focus on *becoming* the type of person you would love to have as a partner. This will help you create a deeply satisfying relationship.

Chapter 14

Having Children

Moving away from our families, literally and metaphorically, creates a vacuum that we seek to fill by developing a close group of friends, aligning with an intimate partner, or starting a family of our own. How does this fit into a calling? Becoming a parent can be a calling in and of itself—perhaps your greatest calling—and an integral part of reaching your potential. You could also be completely devoted to your children, yet also have dreams that do not directly involve them. Or you might feel ambivalent about having children at all, especially while you are still in your twenties.

Although I don't have children, I enjoy listening to the stories of people who do. In a small way, their stories help me absorb the lessons they have learned. Twentysomething parents have told me that their children have brought huge positive changes into their lives. They have helped them to clarify their priorities, to put their previous problems and concerns into perspective, and even to improve their relationships with their own parents. Yet they have also revealed that children can be physically, mentally, emotionally, and financially draining, and that they have had to temporarily put some of their other goals on the back burner. Despite the challenges that children present, however, I've heard time and again that "It's all worth it."

Changes for the Better

Kusuto, a twenty-nine-year-old insurance representative, has become more centered, focused, and fulfilled through becoming a father. Although he had never heard of the word *calling* when I met him, he was instantly clear about his *purpose* in life: making a positive difference in the lives of his wife, two-year-old son, and aging parents. He is happiest when he is spending time with, and caring for, his loved ones.

Kusuto did not always feel a clear sense of direction, though. He grew up in a Tokyo suburb surrounded by a loving family that consisted of his parents, brothers, and grandparents. But he struggled constantly to keep pace with the rigorous Japanese school system. By the age of sixteen, he was going downhill fast. With his parents' encouragement, Kusuto decided to leave Japan to develop a skill that would help him in any future career: English. His parents enrolled him in a boarding school in the United States, where he arrived feeling nervous and insecure because of his low levels of English. With time, however, he made new friends and greatly improved his language skills.

After graduating from high school, Kusuto enrolled in college in the United States. Although he was eager to begin this next stage of his life, he did not adjust well to his newfound freedom after the strict boarding school environment. To make matters worse, he could not decide on a major and he also encountered racism. As a result, Kusuto grew disheartened and depressed. He dropped out of college halfway through and returned to Japan to collect himself.

While he was happy to be back with his family, it no longer felt like home. After all, his knowledge of Japanese language and culture had come to a halt at age sixteen while all of his old friends had moved on with their lives. In search of new friends, Kusuto joined a Japanese social networking site, where the profile of a pretty young American woman from the East Coast caught his eye. Her name was Carly. It turned out that her father had moved her family to Japan for several years when she was young; she had returned to Japan after college to attend animation school. Kusuto wasted no time. He sent her a message, which soon led to phone conversations and their first date at a restaurant.

The pair clicked immediately because they understood each other in a way that few others could. Both had relocated to each other's countries when they were young, and they understood what it felt like to be an outsider. Both spoke fluent English and Japanese. And they even shared several hobbies and interests. Throughout the many motorcycle trips back and forth between his parents' home and Carly's tiny apartment, Kusuto became more and more smitten. It became clear to him that "There was no better person for me than Carly. We were so comfortable together." Kusuto's relationship with his girlfriend breathed new meaning into his life. He felt happier and more relaxed than he had in a long time.

Eventually Kusuto and Carly moved back to the United States, where he finished college and they both found work. They were in their mid-twenties when they got married; soon after the wedding, Carly discovered she was pregnant. Although she was frequently sick throughout her pregnancy, both she and Kusuto were thrilled about the impending birth of their child. From the moment their little boy, Keiden, was born, they adored him completely and decided to raise him to be bilingual.

But as much as they loved their son, the first few months after Keiden's arrival were tough on Carly and Kusuto's relationship. Kusuto worked full time while Carly stayed at home with the baby, and they both suffered from exhaustion and sleep deprivation. "I was so tired from not getting enough sleep and going to my job that I left most of the work for Carly," Kusuto says with regret. "She became angry and frustrated with me, and I understand why. I wish I'd helped her more." In the following months, Carly and Kusuto began to adjust to their new roles as parents. Keiden started sleeping better, so they finally got some rest, and he also started smiling and interacting with them more.

Kusuto has found that the most challenging aspect of being the father of a boisterous toddler is that his life no longer revolves around himself. Paradoxically, the fact that he now must think of others first has led him to his life purpose:

> Before Keiden we could go to restaurants or movies whenever we wanted. Now everything happens on his schedule. But my son has changed everything for the better. He's so important to me and I would do anything to protect him. I think my generation is more focused on "me" and "what do I want" than my parents' generation was. Now that I have a son, I appreciate everything my parents did for me. My purpose is to do the same for my family.

Although Kusuto appreciates his parents in a new way since becoming a father, he has also chosen to break some of the patterns he grew up with, especially those relating to the kind of husband he wants to be. Kusuto's father was a strong provider for his family, but he did not support his wife's dreams to work outside the home. As much as Kusuto's mother loved her family, she always felt creatively stifled and longed to pursue a career in the fashion industry. Coincidentally, Carly has similar ambitions to Kusuto's mother. She dreams of starting her own clothing line one day, and she frequently stays up late into the night designing and sewing her own clothes. Unlike his father, Kusuto feels that an important part of being a good husband is encouraging his wife to follow her dreams. He wants Carly to be fulfilled and supports her artistic development.

Kusuto's sense of "home" has also changed significantly since starting his own family. Although he, Carly, and Keiden are planning to move back to Japan in the future so Kusuto can care for his parents in their old age, creating his own family has defined him in a new way. He is more separate from his parents than he used to be. "I used to feel so comfortable and safe in my house in Japan," he says. "Now I have fun being there, but I don't belong in the same way. My home is with my wife and son now."

As Kusuto has discovered, having children can be a tremendous catalyst for personal growth because we instantly connect to a larger purpose. Suddenly our responsibility is no longer primarily to take care of ourselves; it encompasses looking out for the well-being of our loved ones, too.

As you contemplate starting a family, or how you want to nurture the family you have already started, take some time to reflect on your own upbringing and the way you were parented while you were growing up. By doing so, you will gain clarity about the elements of your family of origin you want to continue and the patterns you want to break. This is also an opportunity to shed light on painful events from the past that need to be addressed so you do not perpetuate a destructive cycle with your own children. At the same time, you may want to develop your own vision for a rewarding family life. As you do, consider the type of relationship you wish to create with your children's mother or father (whether or not you stay together), the core principles you want to guide your parenting, and the way you want to take care of yourself along the way. All of these reflections serve to create a home in which you and your loved ones can safely grow and express your true selves.

Questions to Consider

Do you feel that having children is an integral part of your life purpose? If so, contemplate the following questions:

- How do children fit in with your other life goals?

  - If you do not already have children, is there anything you want to do, accomplish, or become before having them?

- Reflect on your own upbringing and the examples that were set for you.

  - What aspects of your family life do you want to emulate with your own children? What do you want to do differently? Similarly, what patterns do you want to repeat? Which ones do you want to break?

- When it comes to parenting, what core principles are most important to you? In what type of environment do you want to raise your children?

- What are your greatest hopes for your children's future?

Chapter 15

Relationship with Yourself

Beneath the endless flurry of people, activities, and changes that occur in our twenties, the most notable transition we undergo is actually the relationship with ourselves. The way we feel about ourselves is the thread that runs through all of our relationships with others. If we constantly berate ourselves, we are likely to attract people who treat us harshly. If our self-talk is forgiving and we take good care of ourselves, the key people in our lives will approach us with a similar spirit of kindness because we will not allow anything else. As it becomes clear that *we* are the common denominator in all of our relationships with others, the importance of introspection and self-acceptance comes into sharper view.

There are many ways to develop a stronger relationship with yourself. For example, you can take a few minutes to reflect at the beginning and end of each day, practice breathing exercises, meditate, pray, set positive intentions, spend time in nature, create artwork, contemplate the larger direction of your life, pursue the activities you love, observe your self-talk, write in a journal, play music, or just lie in bed and allow your feelings to surface. The key to finding your center is carving out a bit of time each day to simply *be* with yourself.

We are all works in progress, with parts of our personalities evolving steadily forward while other parts struggle to keep pace. As you grow and change, try to adopt a compassionate frame of mind because you will inevitably discover things within yourself that are difficult to look at. If you distract yourself for too long from uncomfortable emotions such as nervousness, sadness, or anger and relate to others through a mask that seems to keep you safe, you are likely to feel dissatisfied in your relationships because you are stifling key elements of yourself. But when you relax your defenses and focus on loving yourself exactly as you are today, you develop a stronger relationship with yourself—which naturally fosters stronger relationships with others.

Cultivating Self-Acceptance

In my twenties I have been learning to remove my own mask and be more truthful and kind with myself. This has not always been easy, but it has led to a shift in the way I feel about myself and communicate with others. One of my teachers in college, Carole, taught me a lesson about communicating authentically that I will never forget. One day she and I got into an extended conversation between classes. I was enjoying talking with her, but since I admired her and viewed her as an "important" person, I felt insecure about taking up her time.

I told her that I should probably let her go, that she must need to get on with her day. She replied that she did not have to leave right away. Sensing my discomfort, she asked me to clarify what I meant. "Well, I'd like to keep talking with you," I said, "but I don't want to take up too much of your time. I feel a little insecure because I'm sure you have more important things to do than talk to me." I shifted uncomfortably, my vulnerability on display. Carole's response was reassuring and supportive. Instead of getting up and leaving, she encouraged me to be more forthright in sharing my emotions with others, as they arise in the moment.

For some this might have been a minor conversation. For me, it unleashed a new perception of myself and how I wanted to operate in the world. Until that point my self-acceptance had been conditional. I approved of the strong parts of my personality but rejected what I perceived as the weaker parts. Something clicked: even though I felt vulnerable at times, I didn't have to expend so much energy hiding these feelings because they are a natural part of being human.

Since that time I have taken more risks to share myself in the moment, as Carole encouraged me to do. In turn, I have drawn many people into my life who mirror the quality of acceptance back to me. I now understand that honest communication with others starts with being honest with myself. At times, it means openly expressing my vulnerable feelings. Ultimately, self-acceptance creates the space for more satisfying relationships with others. Not only does it allow us to express our true selves, but it also allows other people to share who they really are, too.

QUESTIONS TO CONSIDER

- How would you characterize the relationship with yourself?

  - How do you feel when you are all alone with no distractions? At ease? Restless? Depressed?

  - How does the way you feel about yourself affect the way you relate to others and the choices you make? How does it affect the way other people treat you?

- The next time you feel lonely, unhappy, or ill at ease, ask yourself what you need in that moment. Maybe you need to reach out for more support from people you trust. Maybe you need to breathe deeply and allow your feelings to move through you. Or it might be time to identify a thought or behavioral pattern that is not making you happy, and begin turning it around. Brainstorm one small thing you could do to take care of yourself and then follow through as soon as you can.

Part 5

Tools

Living Your Calling

Chapter 16

Mindfulness

The purpose of this chapter is to explore how twentysome-things are learning to experience peace, hear their inner voice, and follow their calling by incorporating mindfulness into their daily lives. To begin, I invite you to try the following exercise. It will bring you into the present moment, which is where your true power lies.

The first thing I want you to do is relax, so find a comfortable place to sit or lie down. If you feel like it, close your eyes. If your legs are crossed, you might want to uncross them. Rest your hands in your lap or by your sides and start to focus on your breath. Your breath is your center, your peace, your entry into the present moment. Simply observe how the oxygen flows in and out, in and out, without trying to control its rhythm or pace. Breathe in...breathe out...and breathe in again. Feel how the air gently enters through your nose, fills up your lungs, and flows back out again into the atmosphere.

Now notice the weight of your body and how completely the chair/bed/ground beneath you supports you. Relax into this support. Beginning with the top of your head, slowly start scanning your body. Do you feel any tightness in your forehead? If so, then breathe into it and let all of the stress and tension flow out as you exhale. Do you feel tension in your eyes? Your jaws? Then breathe into them and let all of the tension flow out as you exhale.

Continue scanning, breathing into, and relaxing into each part of your body. Focus on your neck, your shoulders, your arms, wrists, and hands. Then move to your back, your chest, your stomach, pelvis, thighs, knees, calves, ankles, and feet. Be sure to give your body whatever it needs. You may feel like yawning, stretching, shrugging your shoulders, gently shaking an arm, or rolling your neck slowly from side to side.

Now return your attention to your breath. After a few minutes, shift your attention to your physical senses. Feel the texture of your clothes against your skin. Is it rough? Smooth? Light? Heavy? Constricting? Loose? Does your body feel cold? Hot? Just right? Now let the sounds and smells in your environment slip into your awareness. Can you detect any special odors? What are they? How many different sounds can you identify? Finally, open your eyes and look slowly around the room. Notice all of its shapes, colors, and textures. Also notice the dance of light and shadow surrounding you.

Living in the Present

Meditation is a powerful practice to help cultivate inner peace during the twenties, and at any stage of life. Although meditation is commonly associated with religion, it is not necessary to practice any particular religion in order to develop a practice and reap its benefits. Meditation is personal and experiential. It leads you directly into yourself and can transform your life from the inside out. With regular practice, it also has physical benefits and can help you manage stress, anxiety, and pain more effectively. Various traditions around the world have developed countless meditation techniques. Some of them ask you to focus on your breath; some ask you to repeat a mantra; some ask you to gaze at a candle or an object; some ask you to do visualizations. In this chapter I will focus on a basic type of meditation that can be practiced anytime and anywhere: mindfulness.

Mindfulness, as I experience it, is the practice of gently focusing attention in the "now." You can connect to the present moment no matter where you are, who you are with, or what you are doing. Many twentysomethings already live mindfully in certain areas of their lives, even if they do not use this term to describe their experience. Present moment awareness arises naturally during certain activities such as when you practice a favorite sport, spend an afternoon gardening, take your dog for a walk, play an instrument, or engage in a meaningful conversation with someone you love.

When we are mindful, we are rooted in the immediacy of this moment. We are aware of our breath, thoughts, feelings, physical sensations, and environment. When we are not mindful, the tendency is to become so absorbed in our thoughts that we barely notice anything else. We become "stuck in our heads," which can narrow our world and cause a painful feeling of separation from our environment and other people.

Preoccupation with the past and future creates and magnifies stress. For example, when you ruminate about the future, it is easy to get caught up in worries about what could go wrong; when you obsess about the past, you may relive situations that make you feel angry, guilty, or ashamed. But when you relax into the present moment, you discover the only peace that is ever available. You come home to yourself and claim your own truth. This experience of authenticity lies at the heart of a calling. When you focus your attention in the present moment, you are able to approach life from a centered state of being, make decisions with greater clarity, and develop the strength to follow your inner voice. You are also able to listen to others more fully, without interrupting them or planning out what to say next. This helps you culti- vate deeper, more satisfying relationships.

Through mindfulness, you can cultivate an *observing presence* that lives within you and becomes stronger with practice. This observing presence is the ability to watch your thoughts and feelings pass through without getting so caught up in them that you identify with them. Paradoxically, by learning to observe yourself you can actually participate more fully in your life, and with less conflict. This is because you become rooted in the simplicity of the present moment instead of being thrown around by judgments, worries, assumptions, and turbulent emotions. You are also able to accept feelings of discomfort more readily, without pushing them away or acting them out. As you calm your internal static, you connect to the powerful life force that always flows beneath it.

QUESTIONS TO CONSIDER

- What does meditation mean to you personally?

    □ How are you already living mindfully? Consider the times you are fully rooted in the present moment, when you are aware of your breath, physical sensa- tions, and environment.

    □ What methods do you use now to calm your mind and emotions? Do you have an activity that soothes you such as running, knitting, or listening to music? Do you practice breathing exercises? Yoga? Extreme sports? Or do you maintain a more formal daily med- itation practice?

¤ How would your life and relationships benefit from spending a little more time in a centered state each day?

Storylines

Mindfulness is a particularly helpful tool with which to deepen your understanding of yourself and the world around you. Inherent within any situation are two components: the facts and your interpretation of the facts. Your interpretation is called a *storyline*. A storyline develops whenever you place your assumptions, judgments, and projections (which are largely based on past experiences) onto people and circumstances. Although storylines can cause a great deal of stress, they are little more than a string of thoughts you take seriously and believe to be true.

When you believe a storyline, the tendency is to look for evidence to "prove" its validity. For example, you might call a friend to vent about someone who offended you in the hope that your friend will agree with, and strengthen, your point of view. On the one hand, the facts about certain situations can be very painful, especially when they involve a personal loss, and this suffering deserves our loving care. On the other hand, in many cases our interpretations add to the stress and create interpersonal conflict.

When difficult situations arise, the key is to feel the energy of emotion in your body while observing, rather than getting trapped in, the storylines swimming around in your head. Then ask yourself, "Is my interpretation objectively true?" and consider other ways to look at the situation. If you need help viewing it in another way, consider talking it through with an encouraging friend or confidant. This will help you separate fact from fiction and reclaim your personal power.

After being with her boyfriend, James, for two years, Rachel, twenty-seven, told him she needed space. She was preparing to move to another state to pursue her calling as an artist, and the dynamics in her intimate relationship needed to shift so she could move forward with her life and career. When the separation that she initiated led to a final breakup, Rachel was devastated. To make matters worse, only a couple of weeks later she spotted James looking very friendly with another woman, who quickly became his new girlfriend. This made Rachel feel victimized and it plagued her with painful thoughts: *How could he move on so quickly? Did I make up all of our magical moments? James doesn't care about me. I'm disposable.*

Six weeks later Rachel and James finally had a long heart-to-heart conversation. After weeks of feeling anxious, depressed, and disposable, Rachel was surprised when James confided in her that he was hurting, too. He told her how sad he had been about their breakup, how disappointed he was that they didn't get to do everything they had planned together.

In Rachel's situation, the facts were as follows: she and James had had a two-year relationship; she told him she needed space; they decided to break up; he began seeing someone else soon thereafter. Her interpretation of the facts, or storyline, was: *James doesn't care about me. I'm disposable.* After their conversation, Rachel understood that her belief that James didn't care about her, which had caused her much pain, was not true. Her beliefs were a story produced by her own mind, one that had its roots in wounds long past.

This realization freed Rachel's emotional energy enough to allow her to begin reclaiming her personal power. As she examined her own role in the unraveling of the relationship, she unearthed insecurities in other areas of her life that needed attention if she was to embody the person she wanted to become. To help her get through this difficult time, she adopted several breathing exercises, which she practices a couple of nights a week, and she also started practicing yoga. Slowly, her heart began to heal and she was able to enter the next phase of her life.

STORYLINE EXERCISE

To begin healing a painful situation in your life, try the following exercise. You may even want to write it out.

Call to mind a situation that is causing you pain or stress. Maybe you are going through a difficult breakup, or you were turned down for your dream job, or you are worried about a family member who is seriously ill. Now, identify the basic facts about the situation.

Next, ask yourself, "How am I interpreting these facts?" Pay special attention to the interpretations that are amplifying your pain or stress. Let's say you weren't accepted to your preferred graduate school. You might have a storyline running in your mind that says: *I'm a failure. I'm not good enough. I'll never make money doing what I love.*

Then tune into your breathing and mentally "unhook" from the storyline for just a moment. Close your eyes and focus on your heart. Is your interpretation of this situation objectively true, or are you projecting your own assumptions onto it? What are you feeling? What do you need to be at peace? You might need to look at the situation in a slightly different way. You might feel an impulse to pick up the phone and call someone. Or you might need to exercise to burn off nervous energy. Often the solution simply requires that you sit quietly, feel into the wisdom of your heart, and let the situation *be* without interfering at all. Let your inner voice lead the way.

Meditation in Action

Overall, the broadest application of mindfulness pertains to the way you live your life: the attitudes you hold about yourself, how you treat other people, and the energy you spread into your environment. Therefore, another way to view mindfulness is *meditation in action*. Each moment gives you the opportunity to wake up, allow your natural well-being to flow, and send it into the world.

Hamptony, twenty-eight, grew up in the Dominican Republic. When he was a teenager, his family moved to the United States, plunging him into culture shock: he didn't speak any English and he had only seen white people a few times before at the beach. He spent the next few years feeling like he didn't fit in. In his mid-twenties, he began asking himself the bigger questions: *Who am I? What kind of man am I becoming? What is my purpose?* He reflects on his transformation:

> I was working at an office job and had the feeling, "This is not me. This is not my life." So I quit my job and went to work on an organic farm in Colorado. The whole experience was very healing; I unplugged and re-energized. It was about that time that my compass became oriented in the direction of self-realization.

With his purpose and priorities clarified, Hamptony "stopped wasting time on idleness." He focused on engaging other people in meaningful conversations whenever he could and began reading various spiritual and religious texts. His joy deepened along with his growing awareness. Today, Hamptony is a baker and writer who plans to move back to the Dominican Republic in the future to open a recycling center. He describes his life as meditation in action.

"I make an effort to put beautiful things in my head each day, to brainwash myself with consciousness," he says. Hamptony uses every activity as an opportunity to awaken from his mundane thoughts and enter fully into the present moment. While driving, he listens to recordings by spiritual teachers who calm and inspire him. At work, he stays aware of his breathing and focuses on the process of baking bread: the smells, the textures, the movements. One of Hamptony's favorite pastimes is playing pool. He brings such mindfulness to this activity that he now refers to the pool table as his "little Zen garden."

In addition to yoga, the main meditative activity in Hamptony's life is rock climbing, which he loves largely because it "forces" him into the present moment. "Repositioning a toe a quarter inch or adding a slight twist to my hip can make all the difference," he says. "I have to be totally aligned in my mind, body, and breath. When falling is not an option, only that moment exists." Through his own experience immersing in the present moment, Hamptony has learned about the nature of the human mind. "Most people believe that their mental impulses define who they are. But there's a gap between what happens to us and what we choose to do about it. I try to be aware of the gap."

Tips for Calming Your Mind

As Hamptony illustrates, there are many different ways to incorporate mindfulness into your daily life. My conversations with twentysomethings have revealed that many would love to experience the benefits of a peaceful mind, but they don't know where to begin. Others are convinced that they would fail if they tried to quiet their minds, that their thoughts would run away despite their best efforts to "control" them, and so they don't even try.

In my experience, the purpose of mindfulness is not to stop thinking or even to control your thoughts. The process of calming your mind occurs over time. Mind training is like building a muscle. With regular practice, you can learn to *observe* your thoughts and feelings instead of being automatically tossed around by them. This observation teaches you that your thoughts and feelings are transitory. Although they may contain knowledge and wisdom, they are like tides passing through you and they do not define you. Over time, you will start to catch glimpses of—and then experience ever more fully—your true nature that resides beneath them. The key is to focus your attention in the present moment as often as you can remember to do so.

Below are some tips for calming your mind that have been helpful in my own life. Hopefully they will be helpful for you, too.

Find a community

If you do not already have a daily meditation practice, but you are serious about starting one, I recommend joining a beginner's class. Many people have a difficult time beginning and maintaining a regular meditation practice on their own. This is why the structure and support of an instructor and community can be invaluable. Do some research and check out places such as your local Zen center, university, yoga studio, or church to see what classes are being offered near you.

Set reasonable goals

Examine how you already incorporate mindfulness into your daily life, and build on that. Reflect on the times you are already fully present, such as when you are engaging in your favorite projects and hobbies, spending time with your closest friends, relaxing in nature, walking your dog, or exercising at the gym.

If you want to become more present in your life, look honestly at your lifestyle and personality, and start where you are. Some people find that conscious deep breathing for a few minutes before they fall asleep is all they can commit to. Others go to yoga class once a week. I recommend starting with a daily practice of some sort, if only for one month, to build your "mind" muscle. This might entail a practice of sitting quietly for ten minutes each morning or something as simple as focusing your attention in the present moment every time you brush your teeth.

Finally, be gentle with yourself. For example, don't try to stop thinking altogether; just aim to become more aware of the thoughts that cause you pain and—little by little—shift the way you react to them.

Practice breathing exercises

Breathing exercises are very helpful for calming the mind and body. Below are three simple exercises you could practice when you are stressed at work (you may want to sit in the privacy of your car or in a bathroom stall!) or when you are relaxing at home:

- To practice a basic breathing exercise, count to four (in seconds) while inhaling and exhaling. Allow your abdomen to expand with each inhale. You might find it relaxing to hold your breath for two counts before exhaling.

- To tune into and calm your emotions, breathe deeply into your abdomen while placing one hand on your heart and the other on your lower belly. As you do, release any tension you are holding in your body, such as in your forehead, jaws, or neck.

- To balance your body overall, inhale while closing one nostril with your thumb, and exhale while closing the other nostril with your index finger. Then reverse the pattern.

Observe your storylines

When you become aware that you are feeling agitated, take a moment to stop what you are doing and become still. Consciously separate the facts from your interpretation of them. Then relax into your feelings and tune into your breath and body. Allow your feelings to be okay exactly as they are.

Create a safe space in your mind

When you are feeling relatively calm and relaxed, create a safe space in your mind where you can go whenever stress arises. Visualize yourself in a relaxing environment that is meaningful to you. If you love nature, you might see yourself lying on the beach listening to gentle ocean waves, sitting underneath a beautiful tree, or curled up by a fire in a cozy mountain cabin. Generate a clear and detailed visualization so you can call on it whenever you need emotional relief.

You could also create an affirmation that soothes you and boosts your confidence, such as "I'm calm and at peace" or "All is well." Write your affirmation down and position it where you will see it often; you might want to put it in your wallet or tape it to your bathroom mirror. Repeat it to yourself in times of stress, or as often as you can for a specific period of time, such as two weeks.

Feel your feet

Most of our stress lives upstairs; that is to say, in our minds. Bring your attention down into your feet to ground and center yourself, whether you are walking to the bus stop or sitting at your desk at work.

Tune into your heart

If you are having trouble making a decision, sit quietly and "try on" each choice. While you play with different scenarios in your mind, place your hand over your heart and pay attention to the subtleties of the way each choice feels. Trust in the wisdom of your heart when you make your decision.

Cultivate gratitude

Reflect on the goodness in your life. Write down the people, things, and experiences you are grateful for, as well as the qualities you like about yourself. You might even want to set aside a small amount of time each day to specifically focus on the positive elements in your life, perhaps before eating dinner or while writing in your journal at night. Concentrate on them so fully that you inhabit this feeling of gratitude.

Rest

Take breaks when you need to recharge your batteries, even if it's just strolling around the block in the middle of a workday or stealing a Saturday afternoon nap.

Forgive yourself

Nobody is perfect. When you notice that you're being hard on yourself, stop. Then consciously breathe through your feelings in that moment. To begin turning around negative thoughts about yourself, identify the main belief that is causing you pain and then try to look at yourself from another perspective. You could also reflect on your positive traits and the times you have succeeded in life. Or, think of someone you truly love and let that feeling of well-being wash over you. If you are struggling because you feel you made a mistake, and you need to make amends with someone, do so with a spirit of kindness toward yourself as well as the other person.

Be present wherever you are

Set the intention to be present. Bring mindfulness to your next activity, whether it is as small as doing dishes or talking on the phone. If you are doing dishes, notice the temperature of the water, the sensation of it pouring over your hands, and the texture of the plates. Observe the rhythm of your breath, feel your feet planted on the floor, and listen to the subtle sounds in your environment.

Other ways to be mindful include tasting all of the flavors in your morning tea or coffee, noticing the afternoon breeze on your skin, listening deeply to others without interrupting them, and embracing your feelings without judgment. Stress drops away in the immediacy of the moment, when the mind is focused on the *now* instead of the past or future. Every moment is fresh. Every moment is an opportunity to awaken to your true self.

Chapter 17

Trust

In our culture of instant gratification, it is easy to understand why many of us feel an urgency to figure out the details of our lives *right now*. During our twenties, we want to see into the future of our work, relationships, adventures, and finances. When we feel happy, we want it to last. When we feel unhappy, we want reassurance that everything will turn around. Deep down we know that this decade will be over before we know it, and we fear wasting our time.

Yet despite our best attempts to peer into the future, it stubbornly casts an uncertain shadow. To balance our unsettled emotions, we need a strong dose of trust. But in the face of a faltering economy and global instability, not to mention the throes of our personal dramas, we are left to wonder: what, exactly, should we trust? The answer is that we should trust this moment. Trust that we *are* good enough. And above all, trust our own inner wisdom.

Trust is particularly important in this decade because we are constantly asking, "What's next?" This question points to the perpetual state of transition many of us find ourselves in, brimming with love and loss, excitement and anxiety, hope and fear. Because we encounter so much change in our twenties, we owe it to ourselves to make peace with it. Even though we cannot always see what is coming around the corner, we need to trust that we can handle it and know that it has the potential to lead us to our true selves.

You do not have to push your personal agendas forward with struggle and force. Instead, you can relax into the process and enjoy each step of working toward your goals: the simple pleasures of each day, the people you meet along the way, the personal growth you experience, and the unexpected doors that open for you. The perfect outcomes will come together when you follow your inner guidance, set positive intentions, and stay attuned to the calling in your heart. It's enough to take a chance now and again; when you let go a little, things often work out much better than you could have planned.

Not Knowing

With all of the uncertainty in this decade, the search for straightforward answers to our personal quandaries is understandable. However, there is wisdom in *not knowing*, in walking with life's mysteries and allowing them to unfold in their own time. When you think you have all the answers (or that someone else does), you stop searching and growing. But when you embrace discomfort and follow the questions that arise from deep within yourself, you clear the space to actualize your potential. You also have more energy to give to the world around you.

Allie, twenty-seven, learned to trust the flow of her life by joining the Peace Corps. At age twenty-three, she had a strong intuitive hunch that she should join the organization and serve overseas. But this meant stepping into a world of uncertainty, and she wasn't sure she was ready for it. To begin with, she didn't know what country she would be placed in, what language she would be required to learn, or what the quality of her living conditions would be. Despite her fears,

Allie followed her inner voice and went through the application process. She landed as an agroforestry volunteer in a tiny village in Senegal, which is located in Western Africa. Although she ventured so far outside of her comfort zone that she contemplated going home every single day, she was determined to follow through with her commitment.

Allie's village consisted of huts scattered throughout a barren landscape under a searing hot sun. As soon as she arrived, her life slowed to a crawling pace. While she did spearhead several agricultural projects, her days were far from packed with plans and activities like they had been in the United States. Surrounded by a new culture, new people, and unfamiliar routines, Allie learned to ease into the rhythm of each day rather than try to control it. To build rapport with the villagers, she joined them in their tea-drinking rituals:

> I spent hours sitting with the villagers, drinking tea, not saying a whole lot, just listening. I had so much time on my hands that sometimes I sat under the shade of the mango tree and watched the mangos ripen! I had no choice but to go with the flow.

Immersed in a dramatically different environment, Allie began to observe shifts in her mind and heart that would have permanent ripple effects on her life:

> I had been so self-absorbed up until that point that being present with other people was really new for me. Over time, I became truly at ease. I didn't have to know what to say, or what every interaction meant, or even what I was going to do next. I didn't have many direct answers while I was in the Peace Corps, so I became more aware of myself and my environment.

Allie's experience in Senegal was life-changing, and she returned home with wonderful memories and new friends. One villager even named her baby after Allie. Since returning to the United States, Allie finds she can accept uncertainty to a much greater extent than she did in the past. "I'm okay not knowing a lot of things I clung to before," she says. The ability to surrender to the unknown has been an enormously helpful lesson as she ventures further into her twenties.

Today Allie lives in Boston and is a graduate student of public policy. She brings depth and leadership to her classes because she recognizes the merit in many different points of view. Rather than seeking the security of one "right" answer to the perplexing matters of her personal and professional life, she has the courage to explore many different possibilities to find solutions born of a deeper wisdom.

Trust Exercise

Reflect on a perplexing situation in your life. Perhaps you don't know where your career is going, or you are transitioning into or out of a relationship. Maybe you feel an urge to do something that does not make logical sense. Rather than mentally striving to figure out the answer, sit quietly for a moment and allow the question to enter your heart. You may even want to place your hand over your heart. Then breathe deeply into your abdomen and ask the question that is weighing on you, either silently, out loud, or in writing.

It's okay to feel some anxiety or discomfort as you do so. Simply tune into your breathing and your heart. Then release the question and trust that the answer will come to you in its perfect time and way. Over the next few days, notice if you have any hunches, realizations, or random encounters that give you a feeling of resolution or new insight into your question.

Treasuring Where You Are

Trust is not a fluffy idea, nor is it wishful thinking. Rather, it holds the power to transform your life in an instant by offering you peace of mind. Trust is an emotional release, a state of surrender to the way things are, and the recognition that you are exactly who, what, and where you are supposed to be. You do not need to completely figure out your life in your twenties. Despite appearances, few of us do. Try to be gentle with yourself when you feel lost, confused, afraid, or ashamed; these are normal feelings that are part of growing up. Also catch yourself when you fall into the trap of thinking that you "should" be farther along than you are, or that more elements of your life should have fallen into place by now, or that you don't measure up next to other people. All of these thoughts can prevent you from appreciating your unique path and the good things that are right in front of you.

Instead of wishing you were somewhere else, focus on appreciating where you are today. You can do this by giving thanks for the simplest pleasures of your daily routine: the delicious smell of coffee that greets you in the morning, the crisp autumn air, the friendly smile of a coworker. You can also spend time each day focusing on your successes, perhaps by reflecting on compliments other people pay you, your accomplishments (small or large), and your positive personal traits. After all, today is all you will ever have anyway, so you might as well enjoy it. When you do, the future will take care of itself and unfold in its own beautiful, mysterious way.

Chelsea, twenty-seven, believes that every experience (positive and negative) is valuable because it teaches us lessons that prepare us for our calling. "The twenties are like creating a recipe," she says. "All of the individual ingredients don't amount to much by themselves, but it requires time and patience because the end result is a beautiful dish."

After the death of her father when she was only seven years old, Chelsea learned that every day is precious. The following year, when she was eight, she picked up a book her mother was reading on near-death experiences. She devoured the entire book, captivated by its repeated references to the power of love. The book triggered for Chelsea a commanding vision of her future. She saw that she would grow up to have a wonderful family, and that her ultimate purpose was to become a motivational speaker who would teach others about love.

When Chelsea confided her vision to her mother, her mother pointed out that she would need to have a lot of love in her life to give these talks. This conversation marked the beginning of her awareness of her calling: to embody love and spread it into the world. It also sparked a lifelong passion for public service. Chelsea decided that she would run for public office one day, with the ultimate goal of becoming elected governor of her state.

Even though she awakened to her calling from a young age, Chelsea was not exempt from painful experiences. Seventh grade was a particularly "horrible" year because she was put down by other girls. But she persevered and began to uncover her true self. She realized that being popular was actually about loving other people. "My job was to love everybody and every group, to be friends with everyone." Propelled by her rising inner strength, Chelsea ran for student council president in high school and won.

After high school, she attended a nearby university. Soon after arriving on campus, she sat down in the auditorium to listen to a talk by the student body president, a senior named

Ben. Chelsea was deeply moved by his speech and felt compelled to get to know him better. The two quickly became close friends. Three years later, Ben convinced Chelsea to run for student body president. Heeding his encouragement, Chelsea developed a platform of bringing different campus groups together. Then she organized a campaign and began giving speeches. She was delighted and honored when she won the election.

Chelsea looked for work in government and public service after graduating from college and was even offered a position in Washington, D.C. Feeling the tug to stay closer to home, she decided to decline the offer. However, she was dismayed to find that—due to the tough economy—it was difficult to land her dream job in her own state. Discouraged, she called the owner of a car dealership she had met while serving in student government. He told her she could start selling cars the next day.

Despite her previous successes, Chelsea struggled to settle into her sales position, especially since she was competing against experienced salesmen. She also had moments of frustration when she wondered how this job was helping her reach her larger goals. In hindsight, she now realizes that "The only thing that hurt me in my early twenties was me." Although she could not see it at the time, her job at the car dealership was teaching her the exact skills she needed to grow personally and professionally. "When you're young and trying to find your path," she says, "it's easy to miss the progress you're making and the lessons you're learning." In Chelsea's case, she was learning the importance of approaching life with a "fantastic, strong attitude" as well as the valuable skill of negotiation.

Eventually Chelsea moved on from the car dealership to the mortgage industry, and then to a large financial company. Meanwhile she had fallen in love with her friend, Ben, whom she had met during college. One evening during dinner she nervously blurted out, "I think I'm in love with you." She was overjoyed when Ben admitted that he, too, was interested in exploring a relationship. After four years of dating, Ben staged a secret proposal, to which Chelsea immediately said yes.

Although many aspects of her own life have come together favorably, Chelsea understands firsthand many of the challenges facing twentysomethings. She feels that the biggest struggle is coping with high expectations to accomplish "great things" by the end of this decade. She points out that we have a lot of structure while we are in school, but many of us emerge from this cocoon confused about how to navigate the "real world." As a result, we often cringe on the inside when other people ask us what we are doing with our lives.

To ease the pressures we face in our twenties, Chelsea believes we need to focus on healing our own self-judgment. "Feelings of failure and defeat are inevitable," she says. "Everyone you meet is struggling too. The pain you're feeling is a sign that you *are* going to make a difference. Nurture the good parts of yourself and love yourself through the negatives."

To ease her own struggle with high expectations, Chelsea focuses on appreciating where she is right now and trusting that her future will unfold in its own perfect way:

> We need to treasure where we are, not try to fast-forward through our twenties! I think we often forget that everything prepares us for a larger challenge. There's always something vital to learn right now to prepare you for what's coming. Approach where you are with excitement, because you have no idea what's around the corner.

After building a strong family and career, Chelsea still

intends to run for public office. Unlike many people, she is not jaded by politics. She used to take it personally when people insulted politics and politicians, but now she stays focused on her conviction that we can make a difference when we enter—rather than avoid—corroded systems. And underneath all of her dreams, her calling to extend love into the world fuels her every action. "When you realize what your calling is," she says, "you'll look back and see you've been living it all along."

You Can't Miss Your Calling

Chelsea shows us that the more we focus on loving our lives right now, the happier we will be. Plus, every experience we go through today teaches us lessons that prepare us for what's coming tomorrow. But with all of the day-to-day stressors and anxieties we face, it can be easy to overlook this truth in our own lives. It can be unnerving to chronically doubt ourselves and our choices, to wonder if we are living up to our potential, especially when we are barraged with media images telling us that every young person can—and should— be a star. Sometimes we forget that the only spotlight that truly matters comes from showing up fully in our daily lives. Beneath the ups and downs of work, finances, relationships, and adventures, we are all united by the same core desire: we seek meaning in our daily lives, the sense that we are contributing to something larger than ourselves, the knowledge that we are using our gifts.

The reality is that you cannot miss your calling. Its essence is alive and whole within you right now. You are already being your calling and expressing it in the world as only you can. The notion that your self-worth or life purpose can come from anything or anyone outside of you is an illusion. We each have something valuable to offer the world that no one else can duplicate. When you recognize that your true power always arises from within, you shine ever more brightly and effortlessly widen your impact on the world.

Each of us faces numerous challenges in our twenties, some that even threaten to break us. This is why our task each day is to pour compassion on our self-judgment and nurture ourselves in mind, body, and spirit so we open to the wisdom that lies deep within. Through each change you encounter during this decade, always remember that nothing leaves your life without being replaced with a new surge of growth. It is precisely this growth that leads you to your calling. It sparks the most important transition, which occurs as an internal, ongoing process: the shift from turmoil to peace, anxiety to trust, and confusion to clarity.

Final Question

Return to the essence of your calling, the highest ideal that burns at the core of your being. Just one question remains: how are you already living your calling?

After answering this question, take a moment to breathe deeply and value who, what, and where you are today. Give thanks for the wonderful people and things in your life; give yourself credit for the lessons you are learning and the growth you are experiencing; and go forward with trust in yourself.

Thanks

While writing this book, I have connected with so many wonderful people. Without a doubt, they have been the best part of the entire experience.

I want to extend my deepest gratitude to everyone who agreed to be interviewed for this project, including the people whose stories are not featured in the final book. Your generosity, wisdom, and candor have changed me for the better and filled these pages with life. I feel privileged to know each of you!

A huge thank you goes out to my editors, Clarice Dankers and Elizabeth Lyon. Clarice: Your expert "touch" helped to mold this book from a mere idea in my head to a tangible product, and your heart shone brightly every step of the way. Elizabeth: You've been a constant source of inspiration for me, which means even more than your superb editing skills. It's been a pleasure working with you both.

I also feel tremendous appreciation for everyone who critiqued the manuscript, or portions of it, while it was still a work in progress. Your thoughtful feedback was an essential part of bringing this book into the world. Thank you again!

Next I would like to send heartfelt gratitude to the larger circle of people who have shown me random acts of kindness and support as I've walked this path of becoming a first-time author. Your encouragement means the world to me.

And last but never least, thank you Dan, for absolutely everything.

Notes

1   David Brooks. October 9, 2007. "The Odyssey Years." *The New York Times.*

2   *The Millennials: Americans Born 1977 to 1994, 3rd Edition.* 2006. Ithaca, NY: New Strategist Publications, Inc.

3   U.S. Census Bureau, Census 2000.

4   "Generation Y: The Millennials Ready or Not, Here They Come." 2006. NAS Recruitment Communications. http://www.nasrecruitment.com/talenttips/NASinsights/GenerationY.pdf

5   "Generation Y: The Millennials Ready or Not, Here They Come." 2006. NAS Recruitment Communications. http://www.nasrecruitment.com/talenttips/NASinsights/GenerationY.pdf

6   Alexandra Robbins and Abby Wilner. 2001. *Quarterlife Crisis: The Unique Challenges of Life in Your Twenties.* New York, NY: Tarcher/Putnam.

7   Daniel McGinn. August 27, 2007. "After Virginia Tech." *Newsweek.*

8   "National College Health Assessment: Reference Group Data Report Fall 2007." 2008. Baltimore, MD: American College Health Association. http://www.achancha.org/docs/ACHA-NCHA_Reference_Group_Report_Fall2007.pdf

9   "Wasting the Best and the Brightest: Substance Abuse at America's Colleges and Universities." 2007. New York, NY: The National Center on Addiction and Substance Abuse at Columbia University. http://www.casacolumbia.org

10 "Suicide in the U.S.: Statistics and Prevention." National Institute of Mental Health. NIH Publication No. 06-4594. http://www.nimh.nih.gov/health/publications/suicide-in-the-us-statistics-and-prevention/index.shtml#children

11 Allie Gotlieb. September 26-October 2, 2002. "Buffy's Angels." *Metro.* http://www.metroactive.com/papers/metro/09.26.02/buffy1-0239.html

12 Anya Kamenetz. 2006. *Generation Debt: Why Now Is a Terrible Time to Be Young.* New York, NY: Riverhead Books.

13 "The Spiritual Life of College Students: A National Study of College Students' Search for Meaning and Purpose." 2004. Higher Education Research Institute, Graduate School of Education & Information Studies, University of California, Los Angeles. http://spirituality.ucla.edu/results/index.html

14 Anna Greenberg. 2005. "OMG! How Generation Y Is Redefining Faith in the iPod Era." Reboot. http://www.acbp.net/About/PDF/OMG%20Report%202005.pdf

CPSIA information can be obtained at www.ICGtesting.com
Printed in the USA
LVOW091426090911

245574LV00001B/4/P